New Game New Rules

Success in the 21st Century

W. Michael Allen

Copyright © 2011 © 2013 W. Michael Allen

Paperback

ISBN-13: 978-1484060346

ISBN-10: 1484060342

Also available as a 2nd edition ebook

ASIN: B005FNEVPW

Version 1.4

Direct quotations of 1000 words or less may be used without written permission and are permitted for educational and or review purposes.

This book is dedicated to my grandchildren: Addison and Lucas Naplin, Louis and Blake DeVito plus those yet to be conceived, and their heirs.

Devon,

We wish you success in every aspect of your life.

Love,
Mike & Rhonda

Introduction

Chapter 1 – Globalization, Outsourcing and Offshoring

Chapter 2 – The Financial Crisis

Chapter 3 – Personal Financial Success

Chapter 4 – Success 101

Chapter 5 – Success advice (contributions from across the country)

Chapter 6 – The future & Success in the new world order

Chapter 7 - 2nd Edition Bonus Brainstorming

Chapter 8 – Making your mark on the world

Introduction

This is not a complex book. It uses common straight forward language to summarize difficult subjects. The goal is to give you a quick one or two evening read that you can refer to time and again to plan for success. Research for this book confirmed that there are thousands of pages available on the subjects covered. A quick search on Google or Amazon will offer loads of choices if you want to drill deeper.

The first ten years of the 21st century was an awesome and depressing decade. In the classic words, it was the best of times and it was the worst of times. This past decade will change the way we view the world. We have seen unbelievable advances in technology, and billions of people leaving the depths of poverty to make a real living. At the same time we have seen houses and fortunes lost and millions of Americans become unemployed. Globalization, outsourcing, and offshoring have passed the tipping point. The industrial age is over and manufacturing, while still important in America, is moving towards a role similar to that of agriculture where only a small percentage of the available workforce needs to farm to support our needs. The global financial collapse and bailout is reshaping the information age and the role of government.

Now more than ever success is a new game with new rules. Opportunities that did not exist for the past generation are within reach. No longer does the neighborhood you grew up in limit your potential. A depressed factory town puts no limits on an internet business that serves the globe. There are no excuses; the only limits on your potential are self-imposed. Motivation to define success and set goals is step number one.

We need to reconsider what it will take in the coming years achieve success, it does not have a single definition; it will mean different things to different people. For some, it means wealth and possessions. For others, family and events define success. In fact, since true success also involves continuous growth, what success means to us will evolve as our life goes on. It takes some serious soul-searching to define what success means to us during each phase of our life. You will know you are a success by the feeling you get with each achievement or each passing day, you will feel worthy and at peace with yourself (what I like to call the good glow).

Go to school, work hard, go to college and get your masters - all good advice but not enough in this new world. We must focus our drive early, and not only work harder but work smarter. There is no silver bullet which gives you a single element needed for success. If you search the literature on success, you will find that there is a lot of good, classic advice available that has stood the test of time. Understanding and acting upon the advice will put you on the path to a great life. Leading authors in the field are: Dale Carnegie, Hal Urban, Anthony Robbins, Tom Peters and Steven Covey to name a few. My goal is not to rehash the great material that is already available but to put a fresh spin on approaching success in today's new world.

Many forces are changing the playing field and challenging our ability to succeed. My plan is to give you a better understanding of the current state of the world, the forces at work and how they will influence your ability and your children's ability to succeed. In addition, I hope you will find some value in the success advice I have collected over the years and provided in these pages.

I wrote this book for the busy moms and dads to help their American Kid succeed. The feedback received on the first edition of this book points out that it is not just for our kids. Americans of all ages are hungry for success and have found value in these pages. Like many Americans, I was isolated from the international scene, growing up in a small town in the Midwest. I don't really understand the British, German, Chinese or Ethiopian kids or their needs. If the youth of the world can find some value here fine, but they are more likely to just call me an ugly American who doesn't care about the rest of the world. Truth is I do care, but don't have the background or perspective to advise them how to get on the road to success. The goal of this book is to offer a quick read, a "Cliff Notes" summary without the stories, anecdotes, and quotes from history's great leaders. This book will give a good basic understanding of the forces driving change in our generation (globalization, outsourcing, offshoring, the 2008/2009 financial meltdown, and future predictions). Once you have a grasp of these, you will gain greater insight on success and how it is a new game with new rules. The day is gone where we can leave this to chance. "Whatever will be, will be" is no longer a practical strategy.

The 21st Century will require inspiration, drive and focus. The earlier in life you start on this path the better your results will be, but it is never too late to gain some value. The key value of this book is simplification of knowledge which can help you draw out the insights on how to use the new world situation to succeed. While the original subtitle of the book was "What do we tell the KIDS", the road to success in the next decade is not just for third graders, it is for folks of all ages. Sometime in early elementary school, most of us make choices that have a major impact on the course of our lives. Everyone has to ask themselves; do I want to goof off, play sports and games and just get by with as little effort as possible or do I want to excel and be a success at life? It's natural to ask questions like "what is the meaning of life", "what does it really mean to be a success", and "how can I get the most out of this short time on earth". This is where kids start on a path that guides their development and ultimately their enjoyment of life. Unfortunately it is also the time where many become bitter, cynical smart mouth punks whose chance at success is squashed by their own attitude.

Throughout my professional career, my ability to take a complex subject down to an easy to understand summary is the place I have added the most value. I know how busy life is. For this book to be useful, it needs provide "the bottom line". I have read many books by economists, bankers, futurists and financial columnists - all claiming they are written to give understanding for common folks. While most do avoid in-depth economic theory and the mathematics with their associated buzz words, they don't always shy away from the pompous language that sends us to the dictionary to figure out what they are trying to say. In researching this book, I found tons of material that can give you a good understanding of the driving forces of change in this past decade. For each chapter, I have drawn from my life experience and I have tried to summarize over 2000 pages from current literature in 20 pages or less. If you are looking for an in-depth understanding of any of the key forces of change, just search the subject in your local library or on the Internet and you will find a wealth of information. The promise I make is that when you finish this book, you will be ready to help yourself and your kids succeed in the coming years. You will gain a better understanding of the key forces impacting today's world and how to succeed (because of them, and in spite of them). Start the path to success by having an open and honest discussion with your kids; find out what success means to them. Spark the realization that they can plan for and take steps toward a successful life. For yourself, no matter how old you are, I ask you to choose success and do everything possible to define what success means to you now, and then make it happen. Life will be a lot more rewarding and a lot more fun. It is never too late.

One day in the third or fourth grade, I decided that life was like a game and you could win if you figured out how to play by the rules. It was a simplistic idea but it did have some merit. By then, we all knew that you don't talk in class and don't fight on the playground and "BECAUSE" was not an acceptable answer. I knew there was more involved than just rules to really be successful but most days the rules worked just fine. I followed the rules and finished High School and college at or near the top of my class and spent over 30 years working for major corporations, managing global operations and raising a strong happy family. As I worked on outsourcing and offshoring projects I began to wonder just what are we doing to our kids, what jobs will be left and how can we maintain a dynamic growing standard of living for the next generation. The new problem is that the rules I followed to success have changed significantly in the first decade of this century. In addition to the time-tested route to success, we need to find the new paths and we must realize the new world order will demand some trial and error. It is not a failure to adjust your course and begin again when things don't go well. Bumps in the road are learning experiences. So the hard part we all face is to nail down just what the rules are and how to play the game to the greatest advantage. How you define success will influence which rules are right for you.

The point is that you must choose at an early age to be the best you can be, to get the most out of life. Playing the game by the rules involves being the best you can be in school, college and the workplace. It gives you a chance at being a success. It is the safest route. If you choose this route to success, you need to keep in mind that the most highly successful people probably won't take the safe route. They will invent a product or service, start a business and hire a bunch of well-educated folks to help them run their business. Yes many will fail and end up scratching out a minimum wage existence, the few that succeed will be rich like sports stars. My advice along this line is take the safe route, get a great education become the best of the best in your chosen field and along the way keep your eyes and ears open. If you see the opportunity to go your own way and start a business or service organization give it a try. You can always fall back on your exceptional credentials to get back on track if you fail. Career opportunities have changed significantly over the past 10 years. Globalization has changed the world's competitive landscape; billions of third world folks have taken the first steps out of poverty and started on the path towards joining the successful developed countries of the world. Corporate America, seeking quarterly profits, has taken advantage of this and outsourced or off-shored both professional and hourly jobs in huge quantities. The first thing to get straight here is that I am guilty of calling the companies providing jobs here in the USA, "Corporate America". There are few true "American" companies. Large multinational corporations are traded publicly and owned by folks, governments and pension plans from all corners of the earth. Many employ more people abroad either directly (employees) or indirectly (outsourcing) than they do in the USA. They may hire engineers in India, source call centers in Mexico and use manufacturing labor in China - acting in the best interest of their owners ("stockholders"). Their goal is to produce the highest quality product at the lowest possible cost. The sooner we understand there is no "us" and "them", the better. We are citizens of the world, and while nationalistic pride will be with us forever (or at least until aliens invade) survival is interlinked with the globe. The second edition of this book will arrive on the market in early 2013 and we have seen some interesting changes in the outsourcing arena. Frequently we see news of manufacturing returning to the USA. Quality, supply and delivery logistics and talent of the workforce all influence such decisions. Often return of these jobs results in downward pressure on wages and benefits. Many out of work folks welcome any type of employment even when it barely pays the bills.

Where does all of this leave the "American kid"? Well one thing it does mean is that he/she won't make $30/hr driving a fork lift or punching out parts on a machine press. Those without specialized training or skills will have a very difficult time finding employment that leads to a middle class life style. The remaining manufacturing jobs will pay at most twice minimum wage as will most of the service industry jobs. When jobs do return to American shores the compensation and benefit packages won't resemble those of the past, they will be globally competitive. The scary thing is how this outsourcing trend has expanded to include engineering, programming, computer infrastructure, research and even project development and management. White collar jobs are outsourced at an ever-increasing rate. The knowledge worker is no longer safe. This leads toward the conclusion that to succeed, one has to specialize in college or have a skilled trade that can't be sent overseas.

Having a degree does not equate to employment, it must be an "in demand" degree.

America's strongest niche remains innovation and professional jobs that need a local representative. You may ask yourself what's the use in getting a college education if there are no jobs, especially for the average or below average graduates. The better question is: What chance do you stand in the global economy if you don't have a college education or specialized skill. Better to start thinking now about what field your masters and doctorate should be in and not if you should go to college.

Beyond jobs that need a local presence, we can expect that our national policies will continue to offer an open economy where both U.S. & foreign firms grow and need employees in the USA and around the world; they will offer many jobs in the service sector. Work like legal services, programming, banking and consulting will be in demand. To land a middle class or upper middle-class role in the 21st century it is imperative that you not be "average". You will need to be the best of the best, to secure a good future in this highly competitive world.

Here is a quote I don't agree with: "Success usually comes to those who are too busy and are not looking for it." - Henry David Thoreau. In the past it may have been true, stay busy and you will succeed. The truth is, in today's world you need a plan to succeed. You need to work each day toward your view of success, setting and achieving goals. Engage successful people in conversation, set new goals and work each day on making progress toward those goals.

When you finish this short book my hope is that you will have some new insights and will see your path to success.

While the path will be different for each reader, I pray you latch on to some part of this document. Research it, make it yours, and rise to the top. Life is good, success is fun. Begin now to understand how the rules have changed in the past decade and use those changes to find new routes to success. Global forces are at work with outsourcing, offshoring and the recent financial crisis all will be a factor in shaping the future. Once we have a handle on external forces from the past decade, I will cover the core content of this book - individual success advice - the kind of things that you want to put on flash cards and tape to your mirror. While I acknowledge understanding the past is an important part of charting a successful life, we must also consider the changes coming in the future. I enjoyed reading many books by today's futurists and hope you find this summary of the current thinking on the future helpful. Some future trends are scary; others will make you feel the situation is desperate. Even when you may not like a trend or prediction, you can grab an idea and explore it in-depth and find a way to exploit the trend for your personal success. Success will come your way if you can latch on to a trend or a developmental area that will be in high demand in the years to come. When you reach the end of this book you will be able to speak well on the major forces of change in this past decade, future opportunities, and know how to start formulating a plan for success.

You will be successful following the rules and seeking the newest paths but there is more to consider than just personal success. You can be incredibly successful and still not be happy. You can define what you want to achieve, set goals and work tirelessly toward them and still be unhappy. One must not forget to live fully in each moment of life and take joy in them. Don't get so busy achieving your goals that you forget to live. You are as happy as you choose to be. Include time just for personal happiness in your life plan. It doesn't matter if your fun comes from art, music, reading, crafts, playing or watching sports, or some hobby, be sure to take time, identify and plan for things that make you happy. Enjoyment of life is an important part of success.

I will close the book with some thought-provoking ideas that may lead you to become a success well beyond the average. You can be a success within your own little world or be someone who has a lasting impact on course of humanity and human history. The earlier you chose a direction, the further you can go.

Chapter 1: Globalization, Outsourcing and Offshoring

Globalization

Globalization is a common word now, but just what does it mean? Economic Globalization is often seen as moving jobs from developed countries to lower cost offshore locations. Globalization is more than just jobs - it involves the basic economic and social development of the world. Education, health care, trade, commerce and human services are just a few of the areas where the impact of globalization is changing the fabric of society. To define it, let's first look at two important aspects which together help us give meaning to the aspect of the word I want to cover. This discussion will focus on the social and economic implications of globalization. Economic growth comes with increased trade; social integration comes with the spread of things like movies, TV and fast food (global culture). While the world still retains unique cultures, we are gradually becoming a global society. Globalization has led to a world where there is peace and a growth in rising prosperity. I have heard it said that no two countries that each has a McDonald's franchise have ever gone to war against each other. Increasingly, nations of the world have good economic reasons to solve differences by negotiation.

Why did I start a book to help kids get on the road to success with a chapter on Globalization? It is really quite simple, we are part of the world, and the world is in the middle of a significant change. As my management team sent more and more jobs offshore, I began to wonder just what would be left for my kids and kids all around the country.

You can invent a product, have it manufactured in several countries around the world, and market it globally via the internet. You can find an inexpensive tutor somewhere in the world in just about any subject. With a little research, you can find many differences from country to country, and then just as easily detail how similar we are. The world is truly your playground, no longer is your market limited to nearby towns and states. Competition has heated up; people globally are willing to work for much less than America's minimum wage. Highly skilled workers are available for much less than Americans expect to receive. To secure customers and sell goods, we must innovate, deliver custom solutions and automate or outsource as much of the labor overhead as possible. If you want more detail on how things have changed and the resources that are now available to you globally, read the book "The Four Hour Workweek" by Timothy Ferriss. If you have a high pressure job with huge demands on your time, it is now possible to hire your own personal assistant in India who will keep your calendar and book your travel as well as a research team to create presentations and reports overnight while you sleep. Times have changed - you just have to learn how and when to exploit the changes. Think of it, an average professional working in a corporate setting can afford to personally hire assistance to make him or herself into a superstar (high performer).

Globalization, outsourcing, & offshoring are dirty words in common conversation across the USA. There is a fear of job loss and a fear it is causing a decline of the economy in general. The idea that your task on the manufacturing line, service industry or professional job can now be performed anywhere in the world is a bit scary. How can an American company give our jobs away? How can they expect to have anyone left able to buy their products? The good news is that the facts show that even with extensive outsourcing since 1970, the total number of jobs in the US continue to grow and the mix of jobs today shows that we have better paying jobs today than the ones we lost since 1970. The rise of professional and managerial jobs has far outpaced the loss in manufacturing jobs while the rise in service sector jobs has almost matched the decline in manufacturing jobs. Unfortunately, many of the folks who lost labor intensive jobs probably could not fill the educational and skill requirements for the new professional level jobs. This leads us to conclude they moved to the lower paying service roles - taking a cut in pay and falling out of the middle-class income bracket, toward subsistence employment. Newly educated entrants to the labor market with their fresh skill sets have taken advantage of this change to assume middle and upper middle-class professional roles. Some folks lose and others win as globalization alters the mix of employment opportunities here in America and across the globe.

The take-away as you plan for your success, is that globalization has changed the numbers and types of jobs that are available for the upcoming generations. The earlier in life you understand these changes, the better your chance of coming out on top. The next generation of workers will need substantial skills to earn a middle-class lifestyle. The average high school graduate can no longer expect to find decent paying factory work. A college degree or specialized training will be necessary to achieve financial success.

Globalization a short history:

Globalization is not unique to our generation, it is not new. The true heyday of globalization was in the 1800's. The latest wave of change from a shrinking world (internet, container ships, air freight cargo, cell phones, etc...) is really just continued changes that began soon after humans formed their tribes into kingdoms, and empires that evolved into modern society. What began as simple trade, war and conquest soon evolved into companies and governments taking economic advantage by interacting with many parts of the world. Examples include the spice trade with India and silk from China. Not only did investment flow globally, so did people. Colonists went to America, where they grew tobacco and other crops to send back to England. The railroad and the steam engine opened up trade across America while the steamship sped global marketing of crops and goods.

In the late 1800's, the first transatlantic cable reduced communication time by an order of magnitude. The impact on finance and trade was enormous and created the start of a truly connected global marketplace. We continued in the 1900's to expand and improve communications with innovations of movies, radio, TV, telephones, computers, satellites, and the internet. All of these forces converged to make the world a smaller place where information was and is readily available.

Since about 1980 Globalization has been in the news again, changing the path to success in America in ways that need to be understood to plan your future. Globalization took a big step forward in the 1980's when telecommunication firms strung fiber optics worldwide with capacities way beyond the then current needs. The value of internet based companies soared way beyond their real value and when the "dot.com" bubble burst in the 90's, bankruptcy forced the liquidation of telecommunication assets for pennies on the dollar. Banks and investors lost, as the huge investment in global fiber optics collapsed but the world gained. Suddenly cheap communications became available worldwide. Concurrently, mobile phones quickly became the primary means of communications allowing many countries to bypass the entire phase of infrastructure investment in land lines. In Europe, everyone on the street seemed to have a phone in his ear and the usage soon spread to nearly every corner of the globe. The point is that connectivity has always been a key for strong economic growth and it suddenly became very cheap. Computing went from rooms full of equipment to desktop processors, to laptops, to tablets to phones. Surfing the net can be held in the palm of your hand today.

Overall global levels of business activity are growing at an ever-increasing pace. Every day, thousands of planes are filled with tens of thousands of business men and women flying internationally. If you don't spend time in the major airports like Chicago and NYC, you don't really appreciate the huge number of people traveling on a business mission. The level of activity is amazing. Our success here in the USA interconnects with every corner of the globe; we can't crawl back in a cave and hide.

Living in a small village where the two largest employers, (manufacturing plants) have closed due to global competition, it is hard to see how globalization could have possibly helped the US. Why does the government allow this rape of America, how can the leaders of any US company outsourcing our jobs sleep at night. The answer is that from a big picture perspective when you take into account every aspect of the economy, the USA and the world is better off with globalization. Statements like this one are pretty hard to accept when you have no job; your house is worth less than you owe and unemployment benefits run out. As always change brings with it victims. Displaced people who were blindsided by the fast pace of the global world.

As the 21st Century begins, billions of new capitalists have entered the global workforce including Japan, China and India as well as small nations like Vietnam, Thailand, Serbia and Korea. With a focus on education, these nations have been slowly pulling their citizens out of poverty and toward an expanding role in the global economy. Despite the progress of many countries, billions of other folks are still stuck in countries or regions of countries that have not experienced the benefits of globalization. Their poor performance may come from corrupt governments stealing natural resources and economic aid or just predatory brutal behavior. While not the focus of this book (there are many other books that speak to the needs of the bottom billion), you need to be aware that globalization has not been the solution to everyone's problems. It may be unfair, but there remains much misery in the world. Even with good governance some of the poor countries find that the path out of poverty is a difficult road. Growth is taking many nations out of dire poverty but even where growth occurs, the pace of growth is not keeping up with nations of the developed world, so the gap between the prosperous and the poor widens.

Over the last two generations protestors have taken the world stage on many occasions expounding on the evils of social and economic globalization. The claims they raised span a broad spectrum of sins attributed to globalization and include: mass poverty, infringement on national sovereignty, subversion of democracy, uncontrolled corporate power, environmental destruction, human rights violations, child labor, unfair labor exploitation etc.... There is a vast body of literature that puts these claims to rest. The rally cries are sensationalist claims which are not supported by the facts. The statistics and experiences may show the occasional negative example (child labor making tennis shoes) that can fuel the chants of protestors but by and large the stats support the fact that globalization has been a huge benefit to the world.

There have been problems with the international institutions that are empowered to provide the economic and trade oversight for the globe. The IMF (International Monetary Fund), WTO (World Trade Organization) and the World Bank have all made serious errors while trying to execute their charters. Some of the economic texts I researched built a damming case on how the IMF's failures have caused great damage and actually increased poverty throughout the world. The policies and actions of the international organizations caused great hardship and to this day fuel significant hatred in the developing world. Their behavior has improved during the first decade of the 21st Century, I expect they will they continue to make errors on occasion but they are doing better. One thing is certain, with the help of and in spite of these organizations, globalization will march on and there will continue to be improved economic well-being around the world.

Globalization – The good, bad & ugly

The good: Economists, politicians and most of the educators in global affairs tell us that Globalization is good for the world. The top one billion folks on this planet live in the "developed world" the bottom one billion live in dire poverty of the "third world", in between are about five billion people living in countries where conditions are improving each passing year. The entry of China and India as forces in the world economy has had a dynamic impact on many (not all) in their countries. Exporting manufacturing jobs to the less developed world exported the instability associated with capital investment, manufacturing and demand cycles. This transfer actually provided stable growth and expanding markets in the developed world. It was also was very good for the "developing world" since relying on manufacturing was more stable than reliance on agriculture.

A great example of an industry exploiting the benefits of globalization is the movie industry. US domestic box office receipts have fallen for years as more and more folks buy HD flat screens and set up home movie theaters. However 2011 brought an unprecedented three movies reaching receipts in excess of a billion dollars in their global box office. Among them Pirates of the Caribbean: On Stranger Tides, Transformers: Dark of the Moon and Harry Potter and the Deathly Hallows - Part 2. Much of the world has newfound disposable income and they are enjoying new entertainment options.

The bad: This doesn't mean there were not losers. Workers in the US with only a high school education or less found themselves in the midst of a disaster. Jobs went away, pay went down, and unions went bust. The middle class work force took a double whammy. Technology improvements (robotics, automation) and moving manufacturing jobs offshore hit hard. Over 50% of all manufacturing in the USA evaporated. Unless you see the government move toward a VAT (value added tax) or a strategic national tariff, don't expect to see those middle-class manufacturing jobs come back. Without active government protections of the jobs, it is not economically feasible for companies to source manufacturing jobs here. That means that you need to focus your development toward the upper middle-class (Managerial and Professional jobs) or toward the high-end of "Service" industry jobs (skilled trades). We are seeing some jobs return to the USA, as fuel costs are rising. Many companies are finding it difficult to find and keep quality a offshore management team. In general logistics of foreign production has become difficult for US-based multinational companies. The question remains when jobs do return; "Will the compensation packages be reasonable?". This past year, I have also read of the return of a number of call center/customer service centers to the USA. Satisfaction with foreign speaking customer service is at an all-time low. Companies who value customers are reacting to the perception of poor service and hiring folks whose first language is English for their service centers. Don't get all excited when you read this, press releases are still running about 10 to 1 offshoring versus returning manufacturing or call centers. What this means, is that with some luck, some of the currently unemployed may find a job, but don't base your future on it.

When I grew up back in the 1960's everyone said you needed a college education to succeed. It wasn't true; you could do well for yourself working in America's factories and in labor intensive jobs. Now however, it is true, you need to stand out, a college degree is nice but graduate studies are even better. You need to find a niche, knowledge that others find valuable.

The ugly: Most of the jobs that provided a middle class living in the USA were manufacturing positions and they are gone. We automated and off-shored them out of existence. Most of those jobs will never come back. We dropped trade barriers and protections and pushed hard for free trade worldwide. Now we get to live with the result –

there has been a very big change in the available employment opportunities. Re-education is nearly impossible, only the brightest of the unemployed factory workers will go back to school. Even with a new technical credential they will be lucky to make half as much as their former factory work paid. Since they are starting a new career at the bottom of a career ladder, and competing against students fresh from college. The expanding opportunities in the professional and managerial ranks will likely only benefit their children and highly educated immigrants. The benefits will only come if our children take education very seriously and excel at school. On top of, but secondary to our children's commitment, we have a need for schools to excel at educating the next generation. I would like to pause for a moment and remark on why the need to fix our schools is secondary. If you understand what is at stake, you can get a good education in today's public schools. It requires personal effort and that is always needed no matter how good the school is. The USA is not achieving the results of other developed countries and only part of the blame lies with the schools. We need our kids in high gear motivated to perform. Parents need to set expectations, encourage and reward achievement. Once that happens we need to be sure our schools match their effort.

I would like to think that our government will recognize the need to protect and nurture key strategic industries, but I am not holding my breath for tariffs and tax breaks. I am afraid we will get to watch the Chinese introduce cheap solar panels and other green energy innovations while we fall further behind. With active government protection, we could put the middle-class of America back on track with some important jobs in strategic industries. Until you see America's political parties join forces to create and protect jobs, it will remain an ugly situation for a large segment of our countrymen. India is approaching the need for high-tech workers by developing job specific education - no four-year college degree needed and production can be ramped up quickly. We should consider a similar approach, if not by our high-tech corporations perhaps by an alliance between our educational system and companies with specific skill needs.

Outsourcing and Offshoring

Most major companies are owned publicly. They may have their roots and headquarters in the USA, but their interests and the owners of their stock are global. They care about their employees in India every bit as much as those in Pittsburgh. They are pushed by the stock market to earn growing profits each quarter and are punished by the market when profits don't go as expected. If they can use the connected world (mega container ships, Internet, and global telecommunications) to offer services or build products for lower cost, they must exploit those opportunities or perish.

I spent my professional career working for a global Fortune 100 company in the Information Technology (IT) department. My first experience with outsourcing came in the mid 1990's. I researched the experience of other companies with outsourcing for our CIO. At the time many companies were struggling with contracts which had their IT services provided by others. Most were domestic service agreements with the providers of the outsourcing still using USA employees. My advice was that you outsource to fix a broken service not to save money. Management was certain they could save money and still made savings their focus. Specific measurable service level agreements on well-defined services seemed to be one of the few places where successful contracts were being built. To improve our chance of success our focus was on the well-defined mainframe computer service. Savings was another matter. Usually you could show that the cost of a new outsourcing contract was less than the internal cost but it was a false message. At the time, a well-managed IT service could cut costs 5% or more per year and most contracts were for at least five years. It doesn't take a genius to see that by year three most contracts were a bad deal. The 7% you could save in year one did not match the 15% cost reduction most shops could achieve in three years. The service providers retained the benefits of yearly cost reduction while often increasing the price each year. There is always something unplanned for that needs to be added. Still we decided to outsource mainframe IT services to another US company. These services were well defined and measurable and senior management expected to save considerable amounts by having the "experts" provide the service. The service was provided on site and by year three of the five year deal not only were we not saving money, we held the vendor in default of contract for not providing the promised service. We muddled through years four and five and then moved to a new offsite vendor. 10 years of outsourcing was provided by US vendors with US workers and questionable cost savings. It was an exercise in futility; it was stupid to expect cost savings or service improvement. You get what you pay for and have a lot more control of what you get if you manage it directly. Did we or any of the other Fortune 500 firms who tried outsourcing learn anything? No - we just went global and in our search for savings found PHDs willing to work for ten bucks an hour remotely from India. Profits skimmed by the service providers still make saving money hard and getting quality services from someone else continues to be a challenge. Many of our frustrated customers gave up trying to work through the language barrier and went out on their own to solve IT problems directly.

We went global for IT services around 2005. A major outsourcing of all aspects of IT occurred. A US vendor who had staff worldwide took our contact worth over 100 million dollars per year. Suddenly we were receiving services from IT engineers in India, help desk staff in Costa Rica and mainframe engineers from Canada. Costs were lower and the battle continues to keep service at acceptable levels.

I was part of the management staff that due to outsourcing and mergers eliminated thousands of IT jobs and established the vendor management team. It was a painful process, months and in a few cases, years went by where people were just waiting for their jobs to be eliminated. Our group of six senior managers had no choice but to carry out the will of our executive staff. Anyone who voiced concern about service quality or savings was quickly shown the door. While we did our best to make sure the vendor understood the service required my patience for PHD's who could barely speak English was stretched very thin. The good thing is the staff and management who were displaced found better work elsewhere and left a hostile work environment with a good exit package ($$$). My company saves money each passing quarter and the tradeoff is they sacrifice innovation. Since IT is not considered key to their core mission it may be a good trade. You would think the pressure from top management to cut costs would end but even with over 80% of the services under fixed contract rates they continue to hack and slash in search of savings.

My thoughts on offshoring were "How can my

manufacturing company expect to have customers who can afford their products if they send all these jobs overseas". This would be true if all companies sent all the high-tech and manufacturing jobs overseas but offshore capacity is limited and the US job market is vast. The third world living standards will increase with these new jobs, it doesn't necessarily mean the developed world's standards decline. It is not a one for one trade-off, and the logic of cause and effect does not hold true.

The bottom line is outsourcing both locally and overseas (offshoring) is a valid way to fix a broken service, sometimes it can even save money. The quality of service needs to be managed closely and continuously reviewed. Significant funding (10 to 15% of the contract value needs to be appropriated for internal staff to manage the vendor. Without proper attention not only does service suffer but costs quickly get out of control.

Conclusion:

Here in the USA we are lucky to have been born into the world's top economic tier. Of the seven billion souls on the planet we are among the top one billion living in the "developed" nations. Ok, so you are a US citizen and I say you have won the gene pool lottery. If you happen to be unlucky and hit the dirt poor end of the USA spectrum you will have an uphill battle, but you still have a chance to choose success and make something out of yourself. Yes - at any time any of us can fall into poverty but the social safety net here in the USA will keep us from starvation and at every point of our life we have the chance to decide to turn things around and become successful. Success of course is relative; you pick your target and set your goals. Success could be as simple as food on the table, a roof overhead and a happy well-adjusted family. Or success may be a life of luxury with a six or seven-figure income.

Understanding the forces at work in globalization can lead to personal success. You may find a trend that attracts your interest or a new market for your widget.

Looking back at this past generation of outsourcing and offshoring the number one item on the take-away list is "Don't fear Globalization" it has good points for the USA and the world. If you are worried about the loss of manufacturing or low level customer service and IT jobs, don't waste your time. Those jobs were lost in the past generation and will never come back. Globalization isn't the only factor in the loss of manufacturing jobs, most researchers attribute a large part of the loss to technology and automation and the speed that we automate repetitive work is on the rise. All of these forces that are changing upcoming job opportunities need to be considered as we plan our own future. All indications are that solid job growth will continue in the US economy. You may need to be flexible and willing to move and learn new skills throughout your career, but good work will be available to folks who stand out.

The important thing is to understand the categories of job growth that are expanding now and will be good choices in the future.

Professional Careers – Doctors, Lawyers, Engineers, Pharmacists, Technicians, Marketing, Government

Service Careers – Health care, Transportation, Communications, Utilities, Retail sales, Education, Skilled trades (electricians, plumbers), Food service, and Government services

Managerial careers – MBAs, Business majors

Focus your development activity toward careers that are hard or impossible to move out of the country. Over 70% of the jobs in our economy have a local focus and can never be outsourced. The U.S. economy is one of the largest in the world with lots of opportunity; choose wisely which opportunity to exploit.

Chapter 2 - The Financial Crisis of 2008

The financial crisis wasn't just a downturn it was a complex interaction of financial systems across the globe. It was nearly a total implosion of almost every major economy. How can we hope to tell the kids what happened when the best economic minds on the planet didn't even understand the crisis when it began? It is pretty scary when our leaders ask the academic world for advice and get none. The giants of the financial industry, the university economic leaders and the chairman of the Federal Reserve all had it wrong. Deregulation and letting the free market chart its own course in the world of financial products was an experiment that after years of stability and growth led to disaster.

In the USA we have a tendency to blame events on the President or the political party in control of the House and Senate, yes they all play a role but the fault runs deeper. It was greed that led to taking on more and more risk (leverage) all in pursuit of amassing more and more fees and high returns on risky financial products. If you need to point a finger at the cause of the breakdown you can point in any direction and be correct. The government (past & present), the consumers, the bankers and the financial companies all had central roles. There are so many factors that it is easiest to say the situation is complex and the most valuable benefit we can obtain is the lessons learned. The lessons were not just for the individual consumer but for our bankers, financial czars, and government too. To really understand what happened, you can read a few thousand pages that are in print on the crisis, or settle for my ten page summary. I hope to give you enough information to achieve a high level understanding and for you to be comfortable explaining this to your kids. First off, be aware there are many conflicting accounts of the cause. If you do choose to read more on the crisis be very aware of the date the books were published. A lot of the early books (2008/09) used the crisis to expound on doomsday predictions, socialist solutions, and to just plain bitch on the theft and abuses of the bailout. As time went on more balanced perspectives have been published and I expect a few more are still in the works.

Where do we start and who do we believe? I read many accounts of the recent financial disaster and only time will tell which version of the disaster and the recovery will be considered the correct assessment. I formed an opinion and offer this summary as an easy to understand account of our recent history.

One warning, the world is a complex place and could easily alter course, changing quickly to a future utopia or a decline into chaos. Even though my account tells you that we are on the road to recovery you must stay vigilant and always consider the impact of world-changing events. Be ready to act and alter your personal course to account for changes to the environment and world order. Let us hope that no world-changing events occur any time soon. This century began with terrorism and the horror of planes flying into New York's twin towers, be vigilant for pivotal events like these as they can alter the course of history. If you see a major bank or major government fail or war break out, reassess your investments and plans. Japan's massive 2011 earthquake is one such event; it will change history in the developed world. Protect your investments from a potential default by a powerful sovereign nation. We can all pray that the day never comes when stocking a shelter and buying ammo are the best course of action.

The first thing to keep in mind is that the events of the recent financial crisis are not the end of the world as we know it. The US economy is still the largest economy in the world and clocks in at over four times the size of China. Per person wise it's over seven times the size of China. Our economy has great potential and there is abundant global opportunity. We (USA) are not falling behind; the rest of the world is catching up. Our health (longevity) and per person average income still exceeds all the other large nations of the world. Check out the cool presentation on this at: http://www.gapminder.org/

That's not to say that many folks are not suffering from the disastrous financial mess. A huge number of homes and businesses have been foreclosed upon or just folded up. The stock market and other financial products lost trillions of dollars at the height of the crisis. Now in 2013 the stock market is hitting record highs while at the same time the official unemployment remains near 7%. Add in the underemployed and those who have fallen off the radar and I believe that 15% of our workforce is in dire straits. So far, it is still called a "jobless recovery". Even the growth in managerial and professional positions has been at a standstill. On the low-end of the employment spectrum the minimum wage has fallen in inflation adjusted dollars to the point it is now lower than it was in the 1970's. Low end jobs make it difficult to provide for a family without outside aid or help. The bottom 80% of U.S. families are working harder, longer and often have two or more wage earners in the workforce to make ends meet. That is of course when folks are able to find employment. Not only have we shifted many folks toward subsistence jobs, there has also been a huge income shift toward the richest 1%. We are left with a powder keg capable of derailing the recovery. The real question is, will the inequality in the economy explode or can we siphon off the energy of the masses and put it to better use. The fear in the halls of government is that a double dip recession will take us to the depths of another "Great Depression". The fear should be - will violence and unrest destabilize the very foundations that established this government? Even with deficit spending beyond comprehension, now is not a time to cut safety net programs (welfare). The factor to watch is civil unrest which can spur major changes as it did in the sixties. It can be a powerful force and must be accounted for in both your education choices and investments. We saw again at the end of 2012 our politicians having difficulty with compromise on the fiscal cliff (tax breaks with automatic end points). The real question to ask is how far the economy will slide toward recession/depression before the idiots we have elected do what is right for the nation. If they let it go too far it won't just be a movement to occupy Wall Street it will be dismantle Wall Street. It is a powder keg and a game changer if ignited. Be ready to be super conservative with your investments if civil unrest leads to violent protests in the USA.

Wages have lagged behind productivity increases for the past generation, our consumption mentality and a drive to increase our standard of living was fed not by increased income but by borrowing against the rapidly increasing housing value and funded by easy credit. Now that the housing bubble has burst and credit has become nearly unavailable the world is changed. If you are waiting around for your home value to recover, don't bother. Home prices should gradually recover but it is likely that within our lifetimes they will never again reach the recent peaks. If you don't currently have a home you may be stuck in a position of renting or sharing with relatives. Loans will be difficult to qualify for, and a slowdown of spending will continue to slow growth for several years. Living within our means is no longer a desirable virtue it is a mandate.

While the financial disaster cannot be hung on the backs of consumers there are lessons to be learned. Consumers were not blameless; they made investments in AAA securities that had fabulous rates of return compared to other AAA investments (buyer beware). They agreed to low-cost variable rate mortgages (the cost of which went sky-high when interest rates reset), and spent beyond their means using credit cards and home equity loans. High returns have always met high risk, and spending beyond your income has always been expensive. Since the beginning of recorded history these risks have been recognized as the first steps toward insolvency and sometimes bankruptcy. Taking a mortgage to buy a home is the only way most folks can afford a house. If you lose your job even when you have saved months of cash reserve you are at high risk to lose your house. That is a cold hard fact of life and a risk that everyone accepts to live in their own place. If you agree to a mortgage which can trigger unaffordable payments when interest rates change you can lose your house even while still employed. Don't be a fool with your money, plan for the worst case. Pay a little more for the security of a fixed rate or at least be sure you can afford the highest rate your mortgage can reset to.

In many families our kids have learned quickly that things have changed. Christmas has come and gone a few times with few or no presents under the tree. The latest toy, the new car, and the college education have all become harder to come by. When the family struggles to put food on the table and a roof overhead every luxury and nonessential item is in jeopardy. Depending on your personal level of pain, you may need to tell the kids they are on their own.

Even if you can no longer fund their success financially you can help them build a foundation for a successful life. Help them understand that success is a matter of choice, and how to be successful has not fundamentally changed.

The basics of success are in the "Success 101" chapter 4 of this book. The time you spend with your kids studying success is important. You need to stress that hard work, dedication and a bit of luck, followed by more dedication and commitment will pay off in success dividends. It is not enough to tell the kids that things have changed and times are tough. That is a lesson they will quickly learn, it would be nice to be able to tell them just what caused this crisis and how they might exploit the current situation.

I had hoped that a study of the crisis might lead to finding a solid path toward personal success as we come out of the chaos. Unfortunately there isn't one, success just got harder. The financial sector is a mess; we still teeter on the brink of collapse. In the long run we may look back on these events as the turning point that saved the planet. Our ever-increasing consumption and disregard for spaceship earth has to come to an end. We will go forward at a pace that should give the planet a better chance to survive. Right now for most of us, we have made a downward adjustment to our standard of living, and it is a bitter pill.

The goal of this chapter is to give you a good understanding of what just happened in this financial crisis. Anyone who thinks they can summarize the complex interactions of global finance in a couple of pages is probably a bit nuts. I acknowledge that I am, but my goal is not to create a definitive document with a boat load of footnotes, charts and references. My goal is to make a useful and concise summary. A description of the crisis that doesn't dwell on Derivatives, Credit Default Swaps, Structured Investment Vehicles, executive bonuses and all the multitude of toxic waste created by the financial czars in the back rooms of New York banks.

While reviewing the literature on the financial crisis in great detail, I hoped to understand what caused the meltdown. Weigh that against my recommendations on becoming a success, and to highlight how the playing field has changed.

On the far left you have the ultra-liberal "Socialists" crying that capitalism is flawed, filled with bubbles and busts and has failed once again. Nationalize the banks, tax the rich and build a utopia of social safety net systems. On the far right you have the ultra conservatives saying the democrats relaxed the credit rules, allowing too many low-income folks to buy houses they could not afford, and run up huge credit card debt, causing the collapse of the banking system. Give the upper 2% more tax breaks so they will invest in things that produce jobs.

A more realistic assessment of the crisis falls in between the extremes. In between you have authors pointing out how the greed of the bankers and financial czars created a huge market for fantasy financial products. The underlying basis of many financial products were the creation of investment products that were bundles or groups of sub-prime loans (risky loans unsuitable for purchase by Freddie or Fannie). The biggest banks made huge fees creating products that allowed investors to bet on just about all aspects of the financial markets. This fueled demand for more and more risky loans (subprime loans), which pushed demand for more and more housing all the while it pushed home prices higher and higher. When interest rates rose, adjustable rate mortgages jumped, sometimes double the original payment. Once payments jumped way up, they caused many homes and businesses to go into foreclosure. The housing bubble burst as costs soared and supply exceeded demand, this was followed quickly by plummeting house prices and more foreclosures. Even though subprime loans were only 10 percent of the loan market, when 17 percent of these failed, panic began to strike. Think of it - this mess all began when only 1.7 percent of all mortgages failed. Banks had trouble putting a value on some of the more toxic financial products they had created. These products were based on packages of subprime loans manipulated to have AAA ratings. Almost overnight demand for many of the financial products dried up and their value collapsed and banks started to fail. The banks and insurance companies who insured various financial instruments had created a tangled house of cards and leveraged loan after loan against a pool of loans that could hardly achieve junk bond status. Why did all the legislative regulations and protection fail? It turns out that the financial sector achieved deregulation by buying Congress. If the US Senators were seated by which corporate donors gave them the most money, 57 of the 100 would be in the finance, insurance, real estate section. When you donate the kind of cash these folks did it is pretty easy to see how legislation was passed that let them run wild.

When the failures began, it created a dilemma for the conservative government of George W. Bush. Since the Regan /Thatcher era of 1980 worldwide governments (including both Republican and Democrats here in the U.S.) acted under the mandate of deregulation, encouragement of the free market and global privatization of everything from banks to power and phone companies.

If you study the financial crisis you will see that the house foreclosure problem began in 2007 and was being dealt with (at great cost) by the banking industry. At the same time confidence in the economy was shaky due to a rapid increase in the cost of gasoline (approaching $5/gallon). This rapid rise of gas cost was fueled by speculation on "futures" which the government refused to regulate. The government maintained that the market knew best and they should not interfere. Confidence in the economy began to fail as fear of inflation ran rampant and interest rates started to climb. The whole situation with interlinked loans may have been successfully dispatched by the finance industry if the Lehman Brothers bank had been rescued before it failed. Once it failed however, the global financial system began to implode. Lehman held a central position on many interbank loans and financial products, once those products became worthless the cascade of failures began. Banks worldwide and even sovereign governments watched as their investments vanished. The price of fuel added dread to the desperate situation. Government was the last resort and the only hope to arrest the collapse. Since the Regan/Thatcher days of the 1980's capitalistic governments of the world had pushed for government deregulation and staying out of the "FREE MARKET". The government of the USA stood by trying desperately to support their long held "free market" policies and nearly allowed the world's financial system to collapse to an unrecoverable state. The United Kingdom was the first government to recognize the extent of the problem and throw out the old policies, allowing them to step forward and save their banking system. The rest of the world's governments quickly followed the British lead. Billions of dollars were provided to cover the piles of worthless loans that were built on loans secured by loans on packages of questionable mortgages. Banks that had drained their deposits to stay open were able to continue to do business. New loans, i.e. credit to fuel recovery was still very hard to come by, just staying open was a miracle for most banks. Conservative lending practices still make credit hard to obtain for all but low risk borrowers.

Putting government support behind banks was a major change in political philosophy and will forever change the way we approach economics in the world. It became painfully clear that strong government support of the banking system is required. To maintain stability, regulations are required and government guarantees are essential. Capitalism evolves, new understandings develop and world moves on to increased prosperity. Capitalism will continue to have boom and bust cycles but hopefully not as severe as this past crisis.

There are a lot of accounts of the crisis that point out the waste, and corruption in the banks along with bonuses that were excessive, uncalled for and just plain unjust. My opinion is, go ahead and scream at your congressman, or even get mad at the bankers or businessmen that benefited. Just because they have paid back their loans doesn't make them the good guys. The fact is that our largest banks dealt in toxic assets. I would list them here but I really don't want to deal with their lawsuits. Irresponsible greed, huge bonuses and bad deregulated business practices led to the need for a bail-out of institutions considered too big to fail. Don't reward them by doing business with them. As individuals nothing we do will impact the economic recovery one way or the other, we won't get the money back and no one is going to jail for the abuses (obscene bonuses) anytime soon. Get over it.

I promised not to cloud this book with a bunch of academic

footnotes but I will plug a couple of books. The best description I found on capitalism and what led to crisis is in the book "Capitalism 4.0" by Anatole Kaletsky. It is ironic that in today's global world you find a writer of Russian heritage working at a financial publication in London with such a deep understanding of capitalism. He makes a strong case that capitalism has been permanently transformed by the crisis. He also points a finger at one man whose actions, or I should say inaction, makes him responsible for the severity of the crisis. I won't name names because it really doesn't matter. The one thing I do want to mention from Kaletsky is his discourse on four major trends that have driven the world economy since the early 1990's: the rise of Asia, globalization, the "Great Moderation" (low interest rates, stable growth 1980-2007) and a revolution in finance. The revolution in finance has been broken by the crisis. The other three trends march on. The rise in Asia and Globalization has fueled global growth in all kinds of markets while stability continues worldwide. The game has changed significantly in "Finance". New regulations are in place and we now face a more conservative approach to credit. Meanwhile global opportunities in the worldwide markets for goods and services continue to expand beyond our wildest dreams. There are over three billion new consumers in Asia alone. The second book that I would point you towards is "The Looting of America" by Les Leopold. While this book leans far to the left in proposing very socialist solutions to the crisis it is the single best explanation I have found of the fantasy financial products that brought down our economy. When you finish it you will understand why "Junk" was rated AAA and how the financial markets ("casino") gambled away billions.

To sum it up, deregulation (by both Democrats and Republicans) allowed wild bets and speculation in the financial markets to fuel growth in risky debt. Housing prices climbed and fueled larger and larger packages of loans upon loans. In 2007 inflation became a concern and interest rates rose, when adjustable mortgages reset to higher rates foreclosures exceeded expectations. Then in a move unrelated to housing, investors began speculation in fuel futures and sent the price of fuel sky-high. Highly leveraged loans products began to fail as foreclosures skyrocketed and home prices collapsed. Consumers found themselves jobless or just unable to repay loans as interest rates rose. Many found themselves with loans larger than the then current worth of the homes. Foreclosures made packages of loans worthless, leverage (loan against loan as collateral) of up to 30 times led to disaster as many loan products failed. Deregulation which allowed the business interests of commercial banks to intermingle with consumer banks put savings at risk and allowed such ridiculous leverage positions to occur. As the housing sector fell, a cascade of job losses across many industries made the situation worse. Commercial banks, dealing in financial products (like bundled mortgages) got access to our assets in consumer banks (deposits) via government deregulation (Bill Clinton's administration's repeal of the depression era Glass Segal act). Cash from deposits covered losses, banks became unstable. The normal boom bust cycle found throughout the history of capitalism fell prey to deregulation, greed and the sale of financial products that had high fees and high rates of return, (based on risk that should have had junk status).

Strong global fundamentals remain and much to the surprise of the doomsday predictions the world is on the road to recovery. It is a dangerous path and a wrong step by governments or a major destabilization by other natural or manmade factors could still tilt the scale toward depression but hope of a slow but strong recovery builds with each passing month.

The amount of money printed (created) in the USA to save the banking and financial industry should have caused severe inflation and devaluation of the US dollar. Borrowing from our children's future is a common battle cry to raise the ire of our citizens. So far no financial disaster has occurred, inflation has not run wild and the value of the dollar has not collapsed. Why, we may ask? Well, much of the developed world also stepped forward to save their banking system, (helping to maintain a balance globally) and the US dollar is the currency of trade worldwide, strongly supported with Asia savings. No one in the world can afford to see the dollar fail, and all would like to avoid seeing it fall in value. Can we keep up the deficit spending and continue to bail out financial missteps? That is very doubtful, and very dangerous. Spending beyond our means is likely to lead to stagnation, recession and maybe even a depression. Cutting off funds too early may also result in the same disasters. It is a careful balance and we must rely on a politically motivated government to keep the economy on track. Keep your fingers crossed... despite all the criticism the bail-out is fueling a recovery. If we would have had a balanced budget amendment the experts predict that we would still be in a depression and nearly twice as many would be unemployed. While it sounds prudent to force the government to live within their means there are times when stimulus spending is appropriate and needed. Much to my surprise, the banks have repaid the bailout money; the biggest remaining unpaid debts are with Freddie and Fannie (mortgage guarantee companies now owned by the government).

Capitalism has changed and evolved once again. Capitalism

is going from the pre-crisis era where government intervention in the market was evil and we did our best to let the "Free" market chart its own course, to a post crisis era where we will seek a balance between government regulation and the market. We have seen the need and now have expectations for government protection from the wild free market. Due to factors like globalization, capital is very mobile. It is generally accepted among economists that this makes government's ability to redistribute wealth from the rich to social programs increasingly difficult. What this means to us as people is that we will live with more government regulation, there will be fewer places to make (and lose) wild returns on exotic investments. You will have less opportunity to spend more than you make and will be forced to live within your means. The government will not be in a position to expand social safety nets and we will be more and more on our own to make our own way.

As a nation we need to recognize that if we wish to have new programs like healthcare for everyone we need to raise taxes and/or cut other programs to pay the bill. We spent billions to save the economy from collapse and it is now harder to print money (take out loans) to fund new programs. To make changes like universal healthcare possible, our leaders in government need to make hard choices. They need to consider actions like cutting defense spending, limiting or eliminating litigation on healthcare malpractice, regulating costs and incomes in the healthcare industry, limiting profits of drug companies. Government meddling in private industry, regulations, socialism? Oh my - what is the world coming to! Top that off by upsetting lawyers by limiting litigation -it's a slippery slope and we will just have to wait to see if our politicians can carry out some of the needed changes. There is no choice but to continue with deficit spending (default would destroy the US dollar and ability to borrow funds in the future). The people of the USA understand the need to work toward a balanced budget at a speed that does not stall the economic recovery, let us hope our government does too. In the summer of 2011 both political parties were acting more like children than congressmen by refusing to compromise on the debt ceiling and brought the country to the brink of default. By the time the next election comes along we will forget those that were the biggest idiots and reward their behavior. At least the result is a reduction in the deficit (present and future) and we avoided defaulting on our debts.

Now more than ever it is important to understand how to take control and maximize your success in this new world order. As I think about the complexities of the global financial situation, what do I tell the kids?

Here are some of the facts:

Things have changed, times are tough

Homeowners have suffered huge losses

Businesses have suffered huge losses

Investors in toxic financial products have suffered huge losses

Banks have suffered huge losses, but have recovered with government bailouts.

Stocks suffered huge losses, but are recovering as the economy begins to grow

Credit is tight and hard to obtain but interest rates are low for those who can qualify

In 2010 the recovery began but jobs remain scarce

Four years after the financial crisis jobs are more available and the market is hitting new all-time highs

Not stellar but steady job growth will continue

Income has been stagnant for the past generation

Wealth for the top-tier has grown exponentially

Success for the average Joe is getting harder to achieve

Futurists can help us to focus our goals and improve our lot

Hard work and dedication are still the key to success

Now that is a bunch interrelated random facts. If you think about it, even brainstorm it with a few friends you can expand the list to fill a few pages. Most of us have lived through the crisis and have a good feel for the current state of affairs but often overlook the positive.

Over the past decade:

The USA is still the largest economy in the world, there are opportunities

The global economy is growing (globalization, Asia development)

Over the past ten years the number of foreign students in

U.S. universities has increased by 20 times.

Three billion new consumers have money to both save and spend

Brazil expanded agriculture to feed half the world

Africa is growing twice as fast as the 80's & 90's

Demand for commodities will fuel growth

Technological advancement in the first decade of this century was astronomical.

Internet connectivity is shrinking the world

Cell phones improving connectivity, not only in America but in the back woods --of the third world.

Cars, televisions, computers, and technology have taken leaps forward

Robotics is approaching science fiction levels

Social Networking = connectivity explosion

The worldwide state of human tragedy is being addressed each passing month as global poverty is diminished.

In conclusion:

The financial crisis has brought us tighter credit. Many home owners became renters. More government regulation and the economy will force us to live within our means. There are also fewer places for the boat loads of money that the rich invested in the financial casino (exotic investments). Here are a few examples on how you might exploit these changes to increase your chances of success.

Attract venture capital to invest in rental properties

Expect higher taxes – seek or offer tax shelters

Expect increased fees from banks as their profits will be limited since they have been barred from creating more toxic investments

The financial institutions will do their best to drop government regulation and we must insist our elected officials do not let them run wild again. They may hold the purse strings in reelection campaigns but we hold the votes.

The global economy is strong, even though it is only slowly creating jobs in America. Jump in as an individual proprietor with a product or service. Exploit the global market with the internet.

Create an attractive place for the rich to invest.

Chapter 3 - Keys to personal financial success:

The most significant change in the second edition of this book is here in the chapter on personal finance. It is brief and to the point but is very important and is a concept that was not addressed in the first edition. A large percentage of folks in America have gotten themselves into financial trouble and no system of tracking spending and budgeting is going to solve that problem.

Radio personality and author Dave Ramsey has a couple of books on digging out of a financial hole that I highly recommend. "Total Money Makeover" and "Financial Peace Planner" are the titles. In a nut shell his books recommend that step one in becoming financially solvent is to set up an emergency fund of $500 to $1000. This fund is there to cover the unexpected car expense, the medical emergency, appliance breakdown or just bad luck in general. Step two is listing every debt from the smallest to the largest. Start with the smallest and pay off every single debt, one at a time until they are all gone. Get rid of credit card debt and if you can't manage to pay off your credit card in full each month get rid of the credit cards. Go to a cash and debt card only system to manage your money and live within your means. If you spend your emergency fund go back and restock it before continuing to pay off other debt. Ramsey's books give a lot of detail on how to accomplish a debt free life but that was the one paragraph version to get back on your feet again. Once you are out of the hole the best plan is to take control with the personal fiancé system described in this chapter as your next step.

This chapter the focus is on adults, it is not something we tell the kids but show the kids by implementing a well-controlled personal finance system. In a few short pages I will give you a way to manage your personal finances that can change your life. To be successful you need to set up a simple system to manage your finances. It needs to give critical information to you without taking too many hours each month. With this system you can have a home where money arguments are rare or nonexistent.

The need for a system has been reinforced by the recent financial crisis. It seems to get harder every year to just go ahead without a plan and hope for the best. Before I get started on describing the system there is one simple point I need to make. If you make $300,000/year and spend everything you make you will never be rich. If you make $50,000/year and save and invest $500/month someday you will be rich. It is not what you make but what is left over at the end of the month that determines your long-term wealth.

Keys to personal financial success:

The old saying "Money is the root of all evil" doesn't have to be true at a personal level. Money can cause a lot of stress in a relationship and even for a single wage earner but with proper management it can offer a secure future without constant arguments. I have been married over 30 years and never once had an argument over money.

First and foremost, no system of managing finances will make up for not making enough money to cover your expenses. Your options are:

Make More Money:

Ask for a raise

Find a better job

Find a 2nd job

Work overtime

Sell stuff you don't need

Spend Less Money:

Eliminate expenses

Sell the second car

Sell the vacation home

Cancel services like internet or pay TV

Go to the library instead of the book store

Go on-line for Newspapers & magazines

Reduce expenses

Eat in

Rent a movie instead of a night out

Shop at Goodwill and garage sales

Don't buy "things"

If you can't increase your income you need to decrease your obligations. If you bought too big a house, too nice a car, eat out too often or spend too much on "things" you have to get control at the source. Decide what you need most, sell the rest and try to live within your means. You can trade down in house expense all the way to an apartment or trailer, same with cars; you can go from new and cool to an older but still reliable model. If these ideas don't help or you are not willing to take drastic steps, ask for help. You may qualify for help; ask your local United Way what aid is available in your community and state. There is no shame in taking advantage of the social safety nets that our government and community have in place. (food stamps, home heating credits, aid for dependent children etc...)

Our system to manage personal finances has worked well for us and is based on a six simple concepts.

Know how much income you have each month.

Understand and track where you spend your money.

Follow a strict budget when money is tight. (monthly income and expense are close or overlap)

Never (EVER) spend more than you make.

Plan for and set goals, include long-term ones like retirement, college, weddings and the larger items that give universal benefit for the family (furniture, appliances etc...).

Set aside in personal checking accounts a small percentage of monthly income for each person for spending money.

Now let's explore each of these six areas in a little more depth:

Income:

Before you can have a system for your finances, you must know how much money is coming in each month. No secrets here between spouses – secrets can create money problems via uncertainty and the "unknown". The income we need to know is what is left (take home pay) after taxes have been paid. Most major expenses are paid on a monthly basis (mortgage & car payments, utility bills, groceries etc...) so it makes sense to track and manage expenses monthly. If you are paid a salary it is pretty straight forward to calculate monthly income. If you are paid hourly or are self-employed you may need to track income over a few months to calculate an average monthly income. A variable income adds a little complication to monthly reporting since you can't just show a fixed income, you need to compare expected income to actual income and if you didn't make as much as expected show the negative amount as an expense and if you made more show the positive amount as a gain. If you are lucky enough to have money occasionally come to you that is not a regular income source (bonuses, gifts, art or craft sales, rebates, widget sales etc...) you need to decide each time if the money should go toward regular monthly income to cover everyday expenses or toward long-term goals.

Where the money goes:

A daily, or at a minimum monthly, task is to track your spending. To start, you need to understand the difference between fixed and variable expenses. Fixed expenses are unchanging each month. They include mortgage payments, car payments, insurance payments, property taxes and any other bill that does not vary month to month. They are the kind of bills that must be paid or bad things happen - no choice here - pay up or lose big time. Be wary of fixed expenses that don't get paid each month (car insurance, property taxes and are two good examples). You need to account for these and save to pay for them when the bills come due. Establish a separate savings account and save the right amount each payday to ensure you can pay these when they are due. Promise yourself to NEVER borrow from this account as you are obligated to pay these bills when they come due or suffer those bad consequences like losing your insurance the day before your house burns down or you wreck your car. In addition to bills we also put into our fixed expense savings for goals and planned spending. We put savings for Christmas and Birthday presents into fixed expense so the money is available for the holidays – just like the Christmas Club savings accounts banks offered years ago. The last item we also treat as a fixed expense is funding of a separate checking account for each person to have small amount of personal spending money. Once you have a good handle on your income and fixed expense you will know a very important number. How much is left. You must know just how much cash you can take to the store for gas, groceries, and new things each month.

Variable expenses fluctuate month to month. Major categories include utilities, gasoline, food, phones, misc. hard goods (things), misc. services (doctors, repairmen), internet and TV services. These expenses are more controllable than the fixed expenses – you can turn down the heat, shut off the lights, drive less, cut out premium channels or the pay TV services. If you are frugal you can drive down variable expense but you will not eliminate them since they are essential to your quality of life. You may wish to even track variable expense in two categories: essential (utilities, gas, phones and food) and non-essential (eating out, entertainment, clothing etc...)

After tracking for a while review the data. You may be surprised where your money is going.

Check on the difference between take home income and total expense. Hopefully it is positive. If not you need to increase income or reduce expense. Start by reviewing variable expense they are the easiest to control. Where can you cut back, what can you eliminate? Next move - on to fixed expense. Change insurance companies, raise deductibles, sell assets that generate fixed expenses.

Budget:

When money is tight maintain a strict budget (everyone knows what can be spent on each category every week)

An extreme case here is to establish categories and monthly amounts tracking daily everything that is spent to be sure you do not exceed budget.

A less extreme method is to track spending in retrospect each month after the spending has occurred to be sure that your spending is within reason.

Overspending:

Never ever spend more than you make, unlike the government we can't print money or borrow from China. Overspending can start you on a path that can be very difficult to dig out of.

Always pay any credit card balance in full each month. If you have an unpaid balance you are overspending and have taken out the most expensive loan possible. Pay at least triple the minimum payment each month and pay off the outstanding balance ASAP.

If you can't control credit card spending, cut up and cancel all but one credit card and use cash only

Save one card for emergency use only, hide it away in your dresser or desk, make it a little inconvenient to use. You never know when disaster will strike and you need to pay an insurance deductible on a car wreck, or an unexpected repair comes along, etc... Pay off new balances as quickly as possible.

GOALS

Plan ahead, set goals, save for things that provide universal benefit for the family. (furniture, appliances, TVs, education, weddings etc...). Take some time each year to dream. Each spouse should write down their top ten things they would like to save for, compare notes, compromise on your top five or six and pin them to the fridge or post them next to your bathroom mirror. They need to be kept visible to inspire and motivate you. Take a guess at the cost to fund these goals and decide if you can fund one or more by saving a bit each month. If not don't despair you can always allocate what I call "FOUND MONEY" to your goals. Found Money is unexpected cash, bonuses, rebates, tax returns, gifts etc...

Expenses often vary from month to month. One month you may find you have an extra $500 and move it to your goals savings account. The next month you overspend by $200 and have to take some back. This is not uncommon and is to be expected. Some months by nature are more expensive than others. Utilities or presents or house guests etc... really add up. The important thing here is when you have extra, to sweep the money away, out of the easy to spend checking account. Money left easily available seems to have a life of its own and it quickly disappears.

Spending Money

This may be the last step of my system, but it is probably the most important. This is where money arguments dissolve into non-issues. Even if it is only $10 or $20 a week it is a source for hope and a reward for hard work. It also is a way to control personal spending – the largest source of arguments. Set aside in personal accounts a small amount of spending money from each pay check.

I stress allocation of spending money is the key to the success of my financial management system. The first question I get is how do you decide how much to allocate to each person's personal account. After you remove fixed and variable expense what is left must fund goals and spending money. The ideal range is 5 to 10% of take home pay. You may find years when your mutual interests direct more funds toward your joint goals and less toward personal spending. The important thing is you make it meet your personal needs and review and adjust it at least yearly to meet your current situation.

If your expenses are so tight there is nothing left for personal spending and goals then cut your expenses enough to at least put 5 to $10 per week per person toward personal spending. This is critical to harmony. It's ok to have dreams and goals unfunded but not personal spending.

Decide what spending money is to cover. Clothes? Toys?

Hobbies? Reading material? Individual vacations? Personal stuff, etc... It should include things that are for personal benefit, not food or kids clothes.

Typically spending money should be equal for each spouse but there are cases where you might choose to fund a special interest or hobby of one spouse. For example let's say the lady of the house likes to race stock cars and her spouse supports her hobby. The income left after expenses is adequate to support the $1000/month hobby so rather than each taking $300 per month to cover personal spending he agrees to her taking $1300/month to his $300. This has a couple of advantages, it limits and controls an expensive hobby and allows an interest to be pursued that might not otherwise be possible. If you do decide to have unequal funding, review it every 6 months and maybe even alternate who gets the big benefit.

Another example of unequal funding is to keep things fair and still limit spending to reasonable levels. A professional woman's wardrobe is probably three times as expensive as a man's business wardrobe. To keep wild spending for "needed" clothes under control, determine up front how much can be funded and choose to put an extra hundred or two toward that cause each month.

Never question how someone uses their spending money. The point is to have some discretionary money to spend on whatever is important to that person with no accounting on how or when it is spent. This is not a luxury it is key to minimizing or eliminating arguments over money. Start modest - add to the monthly amount as pay increases come along.

That concludes the short version of my financial management system. The next couple of pages dig a little deeper, provide a few examples and expand on a few of the finer points you might want to consider for your custom version of a financial system. Things like an Emergency fund, retirement planning, and monthly reviews are all worthy to consider including in your system. You need some variation of these ideas to create a custom system that fits your needs.

We have already covered tracking of fixed and variable expense. You can track these by categories and budget what is reasonable for each one or you can simply calculate how much is left after the fixed obligations are cared for and limit your spending to that amount.

For example if your income is $4000 per month and your fixed expenses are $3000 you must limit your variable expense to $1000 by closely tracking spending or only using cash. This can be the end of it, once you know and save for your fixed expense and limit your variable expense to the remaining funds you can proceed with confidence. However, I think it is healthy to actually know where your money is going for variable expenses. Because there may be surprises here, such as $7 a day for a fast food lunch can quickly add up to $200/month. A big part of your income each month is put away in an untouchable account (fixed expense), so the only place you can blow your budget is on variable spending items. That is not to say you should not try to squeeze fixed expenses to a minimum, always be on the lookout for better insurance pricing, lower interest rates on your mortgage, etc... Setting and saving for goals is one of the most rewarding aspects of having financial control.

Everyone's list of variable expense will be different; you track what is important to you. By tracking the common categories you know where most of your money goes, for the odd stuff that comes up use the categories "miscellaneous hard goods" and "miscellaneous services" to track the rest.

Retirement

If your employer offers a 401K use it to save for retirement, save as much as you can spare. The minimum amount should be whatever your company matches. Financial advisors will tell you not to borrow from your 401K. My stand is be careful borrowing from your 401K, taking money out and paying it back with interest can limit the upside growth potential of your savings. Not borrowing from your 401K is correct if you stay fully invested in growth mutual funds however if you are at a point in your investment life that you keep some percent of your 401K in fixed or bond income funds, and your job is safe, you can safely borrow from yourself with no downside impact. The positive impact is a loan to yourself at a good rate. Keep in mind that if you borrow from your 401K and lose your job the loan will become fully due immediately or be considered a disbursement subject to penalties and taxes.

If you do not work for an employer that offers a 401K save in an IRA and even use separate after tax accounts for retirement. If you qualify invest in a Roth IRA (the Roth won't save you any taxes now since it is funded with after tax income). The nice thing is that as the Roth fund earns money it will accumulate tax free and no taxes will be due when you take money out of the fund during retirement. No minimum distributions are required from a Roth so they provide great flexibility.

Review your progress

Every few months the key members of the family should

review the household's financial performance just like a company. During the review the monthly performance is not the only thing that needs to be covered. A discussion of goals and exactly how much is saved for each goal should be covered. New goals should be put on the dream list or even added to the monthly savings plan when everyone agrees.

Emergency Fund

An emergency fund is needed because unexpected expenses do come up and sometimes bad things like job loss occurs or we just don't earn as much as expected. The old rule of thumb is save three months expenses; however in the current economy you should consider your job stability and perhaps save more. Don't sacrifice all of your other savings goals to build the emergency fund. It is ok to take a year or more to save for emergencies.

Create a tracking spreadsheet by listing the categories of expenses you want to track down the left side and list the months across the top

Variable Expense

Phones

Power/gas

Auto gas

Car Repair

Groceries

Meals out and cash

Sat TV, Internet, movies

Misc. Hard goods

Misc. Services

Fixed Expense

Health and Dental

House Payment

Car Payment

Big bills

Spending money

Total Spending

Total income

Leftover to fund goals

There are a couple of ways that I cheat and make tracking easier. I use credit cards for 95% of all purchases spending only between $50 and $100 each month in cash. Rather than track what I spend the cash on I just lump it into the category "Meals out & cash". All of the above tracking is placed in an Excel spreadsheet for the full year. Each month I copy and download credit card spending into a working excel page and then I sort the spending into the various categories. You can establish budgets for each category and work hard to limit spending within your budget.

I create a working spreadsheet each month and use it to add up the spending in each variable category each month. I cut and paste credit card spending into the spreadsheet and then round the amounts up or down and put them in each category I track. The sheet usually has about a 100 lines with entries from credit cards and checks for the month. Microsoft excel spreadsheets work fine for this tracking but you can also do it by hand. Software like Quicken also provides for a tracking system and they can simplify the work required since a lot of credit card companies and banks allow you to download data directly into the software package.

This chapter has shown a simple plan to achieve personal financial success. I recently read a "best seller" book that describes a system very close to the system I have used for the past few decades - "The Family CFO: The Couple's Business Plan for Love and Money" by Mary Claire Allvine and Christine Larson.

This 2004 book is in the bargain bin and at this writing still available used from Amazon, I recommend it highly. The quality of life you can achieve when you leave financial arguments behind is well worth the time invested.

This whole chapter has discussed tracking expenses, knowing where the money goes and how that compares to income. In addition to detailed tracking like this good monthly money management includes tracking the cash flow at a gross level.

Also maintain a spreadsheet that tracks all of the monthly debts in one column and all of the monthly income in another. I list all the credit cards, house and insurance payments, outstanding checks and ATM withdrawals by date due and add them up for the month. I also list the current checking account balance and add in all the income expected for the month in column B. B-A= what is left at the end of the month. This a good sanity check to be sure you have everything covered and don't need drastic action.

In summary:

Know your Income

Track expenses

Save for fixed costs "Big Bills"

Limit variable expenses

Stay within a budget

Never spend more than you make

No matter how small set aside personal spending money

Set goals and save for them

Build up an emergency fund

Save for retirement

Review your progress each month

Track your cash flow to avoid overdrafts

Chapter 4 - Success 101

This book is not about preaching values to you. Everyone must choose what values they hold dear. Once you have a good handle on your values, the search for success becomes much easier. When your values are in conflict with your actions, you won't be happy. The conflicts created when you are not living and developing your values can cause the feeling of incongruity and helplessness. You can still be miserable when you are rich when your actions are in conflict with your values. Defining what your current values are is important; but be very aware that the definition will evolve over time. Brainstorm a list of values and rate them on a scale of 1 to 10 (unimportant to extremely important) this will help you know which have the most meaning to you. Keep a balance by aligning your actions with these values in your quest for success, living in support of your values will bring happiness. An example is of values follows, expand the list with ones that are important to you:

----------------1--------------------5------------------10

Family

Love

Friends

Academic achievement

Rewarding career

Job

Morals – right versus wrong, good verses bad

Children

Dress (style)

Faith

Self-respect

Clear conscience

Worth ethic

Financial stability

Values evolve as our goals and self-image changes. Pick out your top few and set up a success plan to support your values. When you have a decision to make compare how the decision impacts your values. For each of your top values make a list of actions that will help support and develop that value. Remember to reevaluate this list every couple of years to correct your course as necessary. This is where success starts, the rules are next...

Rules for the game of life...

Be the best student you can be.

Every single thing you are taught in school will give you value. You may ask yourself how I will ever use that abstract Geometry or Math proof. The answer is you may not directly. Instead, you may just learn how to approach structured problem solving and the ability to solve weird or complex problems becomes the value.

If you don't understand something, ask for help. If the teacher doesn't help, seek out a student who knows the subject. Dig deeper, study harder; seek out independent sources of information on the subject (internet, library etc...).

Study the skills and techniques of being a great student.

Learn how to read faster, remember more and approach problem solving with a structured process. There are entire books on these subjects read and implement one early in your education and supercharge your results. Check out the course "How to Become a Superstar Student" (Course #140) Taught By Professor Tim McGee, Ph.D., Trinity College, http://www.shopgreatcourses.com/ The list price is over $100, but it is often deeply discounted.

Don't just memorize, learn.

Don't just meet the criteria to get that "A", strive beyond the almighty grade, and seek the underlying knowledge. For example if you memorize how to spell the 30 spelling words for the week, after a month you may have nothing. If you learn the techniques of how to spell, after a month you will still ace the spelling test.

Seek a balance in your life.

Include athletics, fun hobbies, or faith-based activities to fill the time when you are not studying to further your education. Life is fun, enjoy every moment.

Always give 100%, do your best.

It doesn't matter if it is your after school job sweeping floors or the toughest science problem, if you do your very best and someone doesn't like it then, oh well, it's not your problem, you did the best you could. This simple rule eliminates a lot of stress and is important. When someone is critical of you, the first reaction is to get mad or feel bad. If you have done your best and it is not good enough for someone, your reaction is quite different. You can tell them to buzz off there - is nothing more you can do. Or you can tell them you did your best but are willing to implement constructive ideas if they have any. Or you may have learned something from the effort and are willing to try again.

Pick your friends well.

You know the difference between what is right and what is wrong. If your friends share your values, they cannot lead you down the wrong path. If they try, then perhaps they are not the friends you should associate with. It is a tough decision to stick to your own values and walk away from a friendship, but long-term it will serve you well.

Respect and appreciation for people is the fuel that leads to success. Your friends, co-workers, and your team will lead you to achievement beyond what any one person can do. It is hard to beat the collaborative efforts of an effective team.

Superman had it right, live by Truth, Justice and the American Way.

Stick to it.

If you start something finish it. It doesn't matter if it is a science fair project or a season on a sports team. Being a quitter impacts self-esteem.

If you stay up too late, or party too hard and feel like skipping class or work, don't. If you are sick stay home, if you did it to yourself, get out of bed and get on with life - no exceptions.

Think early and often about what kind of work fits you.

What career would you enjoy and feel successful at. When work becomes play you stretch yourself to do more. If you decide your work is a boring pain, it will never be anything more. If you can bring curiosity and playfulness to your work you will find better ways to carry out tasks and gradually move toward better and better jobs.

You need to generate ideas throughout middle school and high school. Once you have an idea, try to explore it. Say you want to be a Vet and care for animals. Ask your local Vet about what it takes to enter the profession, volunteer to intern for free a few hours a week. Try to get a feel for what that career choice means. Research it on the Internet, knowledge is power.

You might find and drop dozens of choices before you find your chosen path. This whole process can save hundreds of hours studying the wrong subjects and paying for the wrong classes. It is important to take investigating future careers very seriously.

Don't be shy about yourself.

When you are following these rules be proud of yourself, be confident in yourself. Strong self-esteem will serve you well.

Never turn down work.

This goes for school and the working world equally. If you are offered an assignment, take it and do your very best. If you need help or resources or need to off load other tasks, ask for help. Don't assume you can't succeed until you have expended 100% of your resources. A lot of failures precede some of the greatest success. Never surrender.

Get-er-done.

You may work long hours at school or in the working world and still always feel behind. You may see others seem to get more done. The truth is they probably do get more done because they have the get-er-done habit.

- Keep a list of every commitment you have made, if the list gets too big rank by importance each item.

- Promptly do the tasks you have committed to. Don't waste a lot of time procrastinating.

- Little things will kill your productivity, so get them out-of-the-way.

- Sometimes you can't always finish all aspects of a task at once. Decide what you can do and then move on to the next most important task. Keep a list of what needs to be done later.

Commitment –

Think of the scientist, the musician, and the sports hero, do you know what separates the good from the great? COMMITMENT. Commitment defines success in any field.

Overcome procrastination

First, start somewhere. Right place or wrong doesn't matter, seize the minute, START.

Second, persistence, once you get going keep going. Always expect the best from yourself. Be open to ideas. Keep at it; you and your team will generate ideas to make things happen.

Third, Plan for the finish. A book, an invention or whatever else – talk about it, see it completed. Once you have a mental picture in your mind you can make it a reality.

To be a success, study and understand what success means to you.

Write down what you will consider a success and then be

willing to plan for and do it. The plan should support the values you hold dear. Success has been achieved across the eons of time there is no reason you can't do it too. "Can do, will do" is an attitude that will serve you well.

Have a positive attitude. Believe always that an opportunity will come to you. Never put away the rose-colored glasses.

Observe everything. Look for and seek opportunities.

Be willing to consider all possible alternatives. A bad attitude can chase opportunity away. You can choose your attitude and approach to life. Attitude is not just about you, it is about what is going on around you, your friends and every aspect of life. A positive attitude brings with it a positive mood and disposition.

Recognize there is no such thing as failure. All things happen for a reason; perhaps what some may consider a failure is really a life lesson. With each setback comes experience.

If you get mad when things go bad, it doesn't advance your cause. Successful people take negative feedback and produce new possibilities and often positive results.

Not everything is fun and games:

A common success factor is forming a habit of doing things that average people do not like to do. In both school and the working world you will find parts of every assignment or job that you dislike. If you choose not to do them because you dislike them, you may handicap yourself. Doing them may make you stand out and be recognized and rewarded for your effort.

In the working world, having just one senior manager who believes in your dedication and talent can supercharge your success.

Remember, you are always free to choose your values, your dedication and every aspect of life.

Don't visualize yourself as a success

Seeing yourself as successful can give you that warm fuzzy feeling and steel your drive. However, it can trick your brain into backing off. Only visualize the completion of unachieved goals when anxiety or fears hamper your progress. Using positive visions can calm you and allow you to restart your efforts.

College advice:

When my daughters were leaving for college I wrote the following bullet points with the hope of helping to make their lives a success. I know it reads like a poem but it has a lot to say.

"If I could give you words of wisdom to build your life around it would be this:"

Search for beauty, the finest experience

Enjoy all life has to give

Appreciate the quiet nights

Relish the excitement & adventure

Reach out and strive to be the best

Appreciate what comes your way

Be quick to respond and slow to judge

Accept those who walk a different path

Do not hesitate to cross swords to defend your ideals

Eliminate fear it can destroy the mind

Set goals, if you want something bad enough you can make it happen

Develop a passion for knowledge

Be honest and fair in all your actions

When you're sad force yourself to think of happy times

Always maintain personal safety, keep your risk taking in the business arena

Save early for a rainy day

Find a way to give something back to this world we call home

Build your faith and know your God.

And the reverse, be happy know your Dog.

~~~~

Let's explore each of these points briefly to understand them better.

Search for beauty, the finest experience

Whether it is a sunset, natures landscape or a person with a kind soul, seek out the beauty in life, let the experience touch you deeply, relish it.

Enjoy all life has to give

Time with friends, time with family, a walk alone in the wilderness, solving a puzzle, studying the wonders of the ancient world, inventing the products of the future - whatever it may be, take the time to enjoy doing it. Look back and give thanks for each day. Laugh, seek humor, and have fun. Life is wonderful.

Appreciate the quiet nights

Don't underestimate the value of a quiet night alone or with your true love doing nothing but enjoying the time to snuggle.

Relish the excitement & adventure

It doesn't matter if it is a wild river raft trip, a trek through the jungles of Thailand or a great book or movie - enjoy every heart pounding minute of the excitement and adventure.

Reach out and strive to be the best

If you always give 100%, you will never look back with regret. Too many folks let apathy, drugs or liquor limit their success, if you are just doing enough to get by, you may never reach your potential.

Appreciate what comes your way

Some things you earn, some things come your way by luck. Sometimes your faith is rewarded, be thankful for whatever you have. Being thankful is a habit you need to develop. If you can let go of complaints and be thankful you will be rewarded, with the glow of how blessed we all are. For one week each night, write down the things you are thankful for the past day. You will be surprised how much there really is and actually start to think differently about life.

Be quick to respond and slow to judge

Have an opinion and don't be afraid to share it, but don't pass a negative judgment on those who have a different opinion or way to do the task at hand. Give everyone a second chance. You may later find that their opinion has merit.

Accept those who walk a different path

It is not your place to judge those who choose to live life differently than you. Whether it's the way they worship God, their sexuality, or they pursue being a super jock or super geek the choice is theirs, accept that they can be good and different.

Do not hesitate to cross swords to defend your ideals

Fight for what you believe in, if you feel strongly speak your mind, gather resources and build your case. True leaders take responsibility for their own actions and the actions of those they lead.

Eliminate fear it can destroy the mind

This is advice from Frank Herbert in the Dune novels. Fear is the mind killer; it can paralyze you and eliminate action. You can't dwell on fear and expect positive results. The best fear can do for you is to encourage you to run away from a bad situation. This action can be a good thing and the best course for survival in some instances, beyond that do not dwell on fear.

Set goals, if you want something bad enough you can make it happen

Few good things happen in life if you don't make a plan. Write down your goals, prioritize the ones that are most important and plan to achieve them. Review your progress every month and revise the goals as needed. There are a lot of books that speak to goal setting, make time to read one.

Develop a passion for knowledge

If you truly have a passion for and enjoy learning you will not just get the top grades you will have the knowledge for life. The rewards are continuous and you will always have something more to do.

Be honest and fair in all your actions

Truth, Justice and the American Way - you have the choice to always tell the truth and be fair in all of your actions. It will build your self-esteem and just plain make you feel great, it is an easy choice to make. It is great to look back on your life and know that all of your friends and co-workers have been able to depend on the fact that you always do what you say, and trust your honesty.

When you're sad force yourself to think of happy times

You are as happy as you choose to be. Life will not always be fun and games, bad things happen, good people get sick and die. Acknowledge that you are sad and that is ok, then list out five happy things associated with the people or things that made you sad and concentrate on them. Count your blessings, even if you have to repeat them a thousand times. You must shed the negative and rid yourself of anxiety. How you choose to face adversity can give you the strength to persevere.

Always maintain personal safety, keep your risk taking in the business arena

Before you jump out of an airplane, take a walk in the ghetto or even walk alone on campus at night – ask yourself if it is worth the risk. Take care of yourself; even consider self-defense classes so you are not helpless if a situation turns tense.

Save early for a rainy day

Start with the first dollar you earn and put some of it away for a rainy day. Put away as much as you can and invest so it can grow. At least 10% will position you to survive life's ups and downs. More is always better.

Find a way to give something back to this world we call home

Make a difference, take on a cause, raise funds, give a kid a chance, create art, write a book, preach to the godless, or build for the homeless. Just do something, or as Nike says so well in sports – "JUST DO IT"

Build your faith and know your God.

I don't care if you are a Christian, a Muslim, a Buddhist or an Atheist. Spend the time to develop and strengthen your faith. Understand what you believe in and why. Always be sure the direction you are being led toward meets your values of truth, justice, honesty, fairness and tolerance of opposing points of view. Be quick to question and dismiss those who propose to change the world through terror or deceit.

And the reverse, be happy know your Dog

While this is a feeble attempt at humor, (DOG is just GOD spelled backwards) a lot can be said for the unrequited love given freely every time your Dog greets you. Be sure to appreciate those moments too.

Sometimes it is nice to keep advice like this nearby. Flash cards taped to your mirror come to mind. You can download and print a set on 4x6 photo paper at this address:

http://success21stcentury.webs.com/flashcards.htm

Chapter 5 - Success advice from across the USA

I asked a number of successful people, just what success advice they would pass along to a youngster who wants to take the world by storm. I received a nice mix of insight and words of wisdom. These contributions are truly from the heart and are well worth study. I offer my sincere thanks to all of the contributors.

Nancy Diment-Wilson – Director - Pharmaceutical Co.

Always act with integrity no matter what is going on around you.

Regardless of the job you have -- work as if it's the job you want. Nothing speaks louder than the results of hard work.

Everyone has an important role and deserves to be treated with dignity and respect, regardless of the title on their door.

My favorite one is "Don't be a Jerk". :-)

Michael Tomes– CPA

All below listed remarks are based on this assumption. "Success is relative". My current definition of success is "contentment". How other's define success will be different.

The rules that I have employed/utilized on life's path to meaningful experiences are:

Manage expectations. Your mind is a powerful tool, which can be conditioned.

Work Hard - (learn to like coffee) Play Hard - (Fun is contagious)

Love someone - Share most things!!

Keep the empathy you were born with, but lose the mundane reflections.

Complete all tasks & deeds because you want to.

Talk to people....

Remember there is not time for everything... Know what there is to do!!

Larry Shelton – Telecommunications Executive and Independent Consultant

Understand what success means to you. Is it money, power, recognition? Is it spiritual understanding of yourself and sharing this understanding with others? Is it personal happiness, a happy and successful family? If these points were placed at the vertices in a triangle, identify the point inside the triangle that gives you the balance point that you define as success in life.

Make sure that what you think and what you do every day

advances your satisfaction that you are getting closer to your goals in all three categories while maintaining balance.

Oh yes, find a lifelong partner and make friends.

Gayle Mateer – VP – eBay

I've thought about it off and on in the hopes that I would have something very profound to say. I wish I did - but in the end I think success comes down to the basics:

Be genuine - do what you say and meet your commitments. If you say you're going to do something - do it. If you can't or don't get it done be honest (no excuses) and commit to a new plan.

Give credit where it's due and take blame when you should. Always acknowledge others who have helped you in your achievements and be prompt to admit when you're wrong or have made a mistake.

Follow the golden rule. It's trite to say that but it's true. Treat others as you would like to be treated, whether they are superiors, subordinates or peers. Someone once told me that none of the perceived status you carry at work with your title, rank, or org size matters when you walk out the door - we all have to pay bills, manage our households, buy groceries, whatever. We're all the same and we should treat others with the same level of respect and consideration.

Be nice. It doesn't cost more. Even when being firm, directive, or delivering hard messages there is no excuse for being a bully. Concentrate on the what and how, not the who.

David Hapman – IT Director

Don't judge others. You don't know what it's like to live in their skin; what challenges they've experienced that made them who/what they've become; their educational background, their beliefs, what challenges or expectations they're facing. Be polite.

Don't try to live up to the expectations of others. They don't know what it's like to live in your skin; what challenges you've experienced that made you who/what you've become, your educational background, your strengths, your fears, your beliefs; what challenges or expectations you're facing, or your ultimate goals.

Live for today. You cannot change what happened yesterday. You cannot predict accurately what will come tomorrow, or how to possibly control it when it comes.

You will make mistakes. There are times when you may be wrong. It's okay. Use these opportunities to enhance your knowledge and education. Search out the new resources necessary to avoid a second occurrence. Thank those who accurately point them out to you and use them as resources for learning. They will admire you for it.

You cannot know everything. Education will occur from cradle to grave, so embrace it and search it out.

Avoid pride & ego as character traits. They are valuable tools for doing a job right and as tools for ensuring your pursuit of knowledge. But as character traits pride & ego will cloud your judgment and lead to errors, mistakes, and potentially insurmountable walls in your relationships.

Sometimes you win by losing. Before you take a position,

ask yourself if debating an issue really matters. Remember, pride & ego.

A criticism is different than a helpful suggestion. Learn to recognize the difference.

Don't pass up an opportunity. It may only come once. Regrets that build up throughout your lifetime can become heavy on your heart and unhealthy.

Time cannot be bought or replaced. How much money you make isn't what you'll remember years from now. Pleasure, enjoyment with others, happiness will not be forgotten. Your work and career goals should be fun but consider whether they should be your primary focus in life. A career helping others may not feel like work.

BARRY R. ROELOFS IT DIRECTOR - GLOBAL INFRASTRUCTURE SERVICES

Do what is Right.

Make sure your word is truly your honor and your reputation.

Never say can't.

Success is defined by how you handle the bad moments, not the good ones. Attitude is everything.

Fear controls everyone, successful people control the fear.

Never underestimate contentment, or security they help you understand individual actions.

Sally Goostrey, Retired – Fortune 100 IT Director

Be careful that, in haste, you don't leave your team behind - you need them with you. Don't try to outsmart them. Success comes with them outsmarting you.

You will not burn out doing something you love. Burn out comes when you aren't having fun anymore.

Life can turn on a dime, other times it turns on a large platter. Either way it turns, fast or slow. You cannot count on it being linear, so don't plan it that way.

Today I can tell you that the best time to walk on the beach to find cool stuff is following a storm after the tide goes out. Yesterday I couldn't tell you that nor did I know to even ask the question because I didn't live on the ocean. Who we are and what we know changes daily.

Always seek new questions, not just answers.

Don't forget to breathe.

Laura Naplin – Marketing – Breakfast mfg.

Build Relationships with Everyone:

- For me, this one has helped me the most in my career. Having someone in a good word for you is in-valuable in your career. This could help you get an interview, but can also help you move up the latter in your current job.

- A few things that I have found that helped in this area-

Smile! It's the easiest way to make yourself more approachable. Another hint in this area is to not stand with your arms crossed as it automatically makes you seem unfriendly.

Try to find something that THEY want to talk about. People love to talk about themselves and love it when others want to listen.

Be nice to everyone. You never know when that one person you met three years ago will call you up one day with a job offer.

Always deliver your best work.

- Your work is a reflection of you, and you never know who is going to read it. Ensure you double or even triple check everything you deliver to ensure its error free, the grammar and spelling are correct, along with providing any additional insight beyond what is typically expected.

Talk about career development with your boss

- You are ultimately the driver of your career, no one else. When you have reviews with your boss, don't be afraid to ask about the steps needed to move to the next level.

Jason Matthews – Author

Events in my life tend to work out better, smoother, and more successfully when I follow the simply daily things that appear to be laid out before me. You could call it karma or universal intelligence or God, but labeling it is getting off the point. Often my mind and ego have one idea for what success is; that usually involves money and acclaim. But when I follow the simple work I have before me each day, the successes are smaller and simpler things that are more meaningful. Maybe it's coaching a kid in soccer, helping my daughter with homework, going to the gym for exercise, participating in a forum or helping a new author. I have a feeling those successes will be far more meaningful when I look back on my life than how much money I made.

Rodney Chase – Retired educator – College Professor/Math Department Head

Just a couple of thoughts from my many years of experience. You had asked one time while we were talking what was the most important advice that we could pass on to the youth of the country. I feel that having a positive work ethic is the most important attribute. Regardless of what your job is you should always do it to the best of your ability and as fast as you can and not try to find ways to take as long as possible to finish the job. When the task is completed you should look for what else needs to be done and do it. Don't wait around until someone tells you what needs to be done take the initiative. This applies to all jobs if you are a floor sweeper be the best and fastest one around. If you are flipping burgers be the best and fastest burger flipper and when there is a down time in flipping use that time to restock the area or do extra clean up in the kitchen.

My other thought is that the education system in the U.S. is in deep trouble. The emphasis on learning has been replaced by only wanting a good grade for the course. 50 years ago if you were going to college it was expected that you would have taken 4 years of math. 4 years of English, 4 years of social studies, and 4 years of science so that you would be a well-rounded individual. No more, now students are allowed to major in business or art or who knows what in high school. Over the years we have had a dumbing down of the courses we offer in all areas so the students will not get a poor grade. Look at a text book today and compare it to one of 10 to 15 years ago and you will find that the material covered and the difficulty of the problems is much easier today. If a teacher in college runs the class for the full length of time the students feel they are being imposed upon, they would much rather you cut the class time in half. The respect for education has decreased substantially over the years. In the old days if you got in trouble at school that would only be half the trouble you would be in at home. Now the parents, for the most part, blame the teacher or the school if there is a problem because it could never be their child. I have said that if they really wanted to improve the public school system what the state should do is guarantee a high school education to all but they should be told that for this they are allowed only one mistake (causing a problem in school) on the second mistake they are kicked out of the public system and their parents are responsible to the provide the rest of their education.

~~~~

Chapter 6 - Success in the new world order

What does the future hold? How many times have you heard "I wish I had a crystal ball"? Well we do have a crystal ball; we just have to use it. An important literary subject covers speculation and prediction of the future. If we want to tell our kids how to succeed, a bit of insight on the future is invaluable. In this short chapter I will touch on the highlights predicted for our near term future.

Some major changes are expected in the next 50 years that will change how our kids live and work. Taking these trends into account is important in planning for success.

The Future

In the 1980's "Megatrends" co-authors John Naisbitt and Patricia Aburdene heralded the dawn of the information age and the booming information economy, high-tech and high touch, work from anywhere lifestyle. It practically became the blueprint for deployment of the information age. In her 2005 book Megatrends 2010, Patricia Aburdene zooms in on a rising new corporate trend: The quest for morals in business has become a rising importance for consumers, they are willing to pay a little more for "green", they expect ethical conduct, balance, hug your customer treatment. When times are tough, people seek good behavior from their own companies and those who they do business with. Corporate Social Responsibility – CSR is a buzz word you need to take to your employer and the folks you spend your money with. She describes this drive toward corporate morality as the presence of the "SPIRIT" and cites a lot of examples where doing the "right thing" turned out to also be the most profitable thing.

Patricia cites seven trends but they all feel like the same driving force – a new awareness for ethical, moral behavior. Woe to the firm caught cheating their customers and treating employees badly. Praise to those firms who show the goodness of the Divine Spirit. This leads to the number one piece of success advice; do your best to be a "GOOD" person. No matter how dire the sweeping trends of this era are, you can have good health and a sense of wellbeing by striving to do the right thing. Doing good at the corporate, national and international level starts with each individual. The spiritual and emotional health that comes with doing good is the only reward you need for self-fulfillment. While this trend is important it has not totally enveloped the business world. Walmart is evidence that cost does matter. With low wages and benefits and goods sourced from China customers have embraced their low cost.

When I was growing up we had Alvin Toffler author of "Future Shock" and the "Third Wave" and John Naisbitt author of "Megatrends" - both gave me a piece of the vision of how to be successful. I look back and say thank you for the insight, it helped make me successful and enjoy a great career in global Information Technology. Today, we have a new group of "seers" trying to make sense out of a world whose pace of change has accelerated beyond belief. For those of us who huddled around a grainy black and white TV picture of the first man walking on the moon, this rapid pace gives cause for both concern and hope.

As I researched this chapter, my goal was to find what the visionaries had to say that might help today's kids plan for success in the 21st century. They have identified trends large and small that will have an impact on the future. You need to keep in mind that even the scary trends can be exploited and lead to a successful career. This chapter will hit the high points of what they have to say and I hope spark an interest in researching several of these subjects. After the next few pages you will be able to speak reasonably well on where this world is heading, just keep in mind there is a whole body of literature worthy of your time and study.

Kids today have some important decisions to make on future careers. Should they look for something safe that can't be outsourced, or taken over by a machine? Or should they risk trying to ride the wave of one of these big trends to incredible success? One thing is for sure, in the USA, it will be difficult for the average worker to make a middle class life style. If you are not in the top quartile in intellect or talent, then you will need a strong vision. With vision you will have an edge that can propel you into the new 'American Dream'. Notice I said 'new', that's because even the 'American Dream' is changing for the 21st century. What we could not imagine has become commonplace, and what we could never hope to do is now possible. Technology and connectivity with the world has opened many new doors.

Now let's get on with what the 'seers' have to say about our future. Keep in mind projections on important future trends assume that the world continues on track with no game changers like an asteroid impact, super volcano, worldwide epidemic, or alien invasion etc...

The six big trends that I found during my review of the futurist literature are:

Technology explosion

Globalization

Population explosion

Scarce resources

Climate change

The rise of the individual.

1. Technology:

The breakthrough technology of today includes computers, laptops, netbooks, iPads, iPhones, robotics, artificial intelligence, communications, satellite services, flat screen TV, computer generated special effects, to just name a few. When I began college in 1973, the state of the art mainframe filled an entire room and took punch cards for input and processed a whopping four million instructions per second (4 MIPS). Today the iPhone has more processing power. The top of the line laptop in 2011 has more processing capacity than existed in the world when we put a man on the moon. When the first Star Wars movie came out in 1977 and when all the Star Trek movies were made in the 1980's the movie special effects were achieved by filming large models, today more believable spaceships are created with computer generated special effects. The sets of entire TV series like "Sanctuary" are filmed on "green screen" and the cool old mansion is added in later.

When GM first introduced robots in the factory, for every robot that replaced a person it required two people to keep it repaired adjusted and programmed. It wasn't very cost-effective, but they kept at it and now as more and more generations of robotics have been deployed, robots are the first choice for repetitive factory jobs. They don't take breaks, vacations or create long-term benefit liabilities and will work as many shifts as needed. (Those great jobs are gone and will never come back for humans.)

The point is technology is advancing on a parabolic curve and we have only started up the slope. The technology miracles we have seen in the past 30 years are just the tip of the iceberg. We will see computers smarter than humans, absolutely. In fact in 2011 we saw an IBM computer named Watson beat the two best 'Jeopardy' players of all time. The goal of this exercise was to test the logic that would allow a computer to answer an open-ended question similar to what a patient might ask a doctor. Think of where this technology could take us.

Today's computers and robotics challenge both the factory workers and the college educated knowledge workers that hold repetitive jobs. If you are going to skip college the safest route to the 'American Dream' is a skilled trade. Electrician, plumber, computer installation and repair, robotics installation and repair, and mechanic (auto/truck) to name a few. As more and more college capable kids choose instead the safety of a skilled trade, competition for positions will be strong. The average worker will find a skilled trade is a path to break away from the minimal wage service sector jobs. Service sector jobs are jobs where you need two or more of them to even achieve a lower middle class standard of living. (Retail sales, cashiers, office clerks, food prep and serve, fast food, customer service reps, bookkeepers, secretaries, sales representatives, janitors, maids...)

Of the six trends we will discuss in this chapter, technology advances will be the one to have the most impact on people here in the USA. If you would like to read an entire book on this amazing subject I recommend 'Lights in the Tunnel' by Martin Ford. Mr. Ford builds a strong case for the good and evil of technological change. He even concludes with some interesting ways to lessen the impact on the average 'Joe'. While his solutions are radical by today's standards they should give our Senators and Congressmen a little food for thought.

Keep the faith; you will need to ride the wave of advancing technology to avoid being crushed by it. New tech will create a large variety of new opportunities you just need to be vigilant, aware and ready to take advantage of those opportunities when they present themselves. Keep abreast of what is coming out and keep your skill sets up to date so you can exploit the technology.

2. Globalization

The first chapter covered globalization over the past 10 to 15 years. But it doesn't end there - globalization will continue to have impact over the next 50 years. The literature on this subject is vast and there are points I didn't cover in the chapter on Globalization/outsourcing. So I will hit a few extra points in this discussion of future trends, you will find an additional take-away that is of value.

Globalization 2013 and beyond

One of the globalization challenges the US now faces after the 2008 financial crisis is to carefully balance protectionism with the expanding free market. The role of government has changed in the economy we now understand the government is the last source of guarantee for the banking system and risk must be regulated in the financial marketplace by the government. Fears that regulation will stifle innovation and force business offshore are no longer valid. The prudent investor welcomes the increased role of government and the security it adds to the financial marketplace. The need grows to expand protection to industry. We must define strategic manufacturing, (high tech industry, green technology like solar, wind, hydrogen) and we need to protect and nurture it. Free trade has been on the lips of every economist since 1970, the holy grail of globalization. It is so ingrained in government that reversing the trend to save our middle class – the average worker has become difficult if not impossible.

Unless by some miracle our government recognizes the plight of our displaced middle class and takes action to protect infant and strategic industries we will lose a generation. We can gear up to educate the next generation for success, but a whole bunch of productive folks will eke out a living in service jobs and burden social welfare programs. We will see some manufacturing return to the USA as global labor and transportation costs rise. When jobs do return the pressure will be on to maintain low wages and minimal benefits while automation will continue to squeeze out more people. President Obama is calling for more manufacturing jobs but voicing the need is not enough to save the middle class. A lot of folks will agree and welcome that their situation is gaining understanding at the highest levels. It is only empty words until actual legislation to protect strategic industries is enacted. We have pushed free trade for so long that there are now barriers to protecting any industry. It is time to ignore the sanctions, break the treaties and use our economic might to rebuild quality middle-class jobs. Action is required before our economic might becomes a permanent economic plight.

Within America our most evident source of competitive advantage is innovation and a deep understanding of our consumer culture. To succeed we must understand what our customers want and need before they even realize it themselves. The more we can customize and build to order, to meet our customers' needs, the more indispensable we become.

The literature on globalization is vast and it's interaction with our future is complex, for the rest of this section I have provided bullet points to highlight some of the things we can expect. When you review a list like this ask yourself what each bullet point means to you, how could you exploit it to offer a product or service. Take notes of any ideas that hit you while reading this section.

- Depending on your skills and education, Globalization can kick your butt. It may be good for global poverty but it can also send the under skilled and under educated into poverty. Stick to education or get back to it if you find yourself short on skills.
- Over the next 40 years world prosperity will improve, you will even see some of the jobs that went offshore come back home. Globalization is too big for any one country to harness and change to any significant degree.
- The world will become more globalized as time goes on. Barring disaster, growth of the world economy will continue. The expansion of the global economy provides benefits to everyone and won't be denied continued growth. Neither people nor governments can put on the brakes
- Governmental ability to redistribute wealth using progressive taxes is diminished by the increased mobility of capital and products. Lately I have

noticed the liberal outrage at the wealth of the top 1% in America. They took all the benefit from productivity improvement and left the middle-class wages to stagnate. This means that if a government comes up with a new tax to redistribute wealth from the corporations or the rich to the poor it won't work. They will just take their wealth to a country that is not so unfriendly. Don't expect expansion of the social safety net.

- Opportunities abound and are not equally available to everyone.
- Globalization has brought the world economy together for billions of folks (the marketplace is huge and growing).
- Billions are still left living on a dollar or two a day with a slow road to success in the future and the gap widens each year.
- The sole proprietor has nearly the same access to the world that a huge corporation has.
- Language differences still complicate exploiting global information but education continues to reduce this barrier
- Global collaboration is now enabled via the internet
- As the world goes toward a more global society, nations, culture and language will still have a place.
- Humans find pride and a sense of belonging within their historic nation state.
- Innovation will rule in the next century and be a source of competitive advantage
- A high value activity is understanding your customers. Speed of delivery and customization is most easily provided at a local level, built to order and on time delivery will be important. We will value services highly as they become customized to

meet our needs.
- Distance will always matter for high touch activities (healthcare, people care, vacations, and services of all kinds), but distance won't matter for information based services.
- The internet and high quality communications has made it possible to hire a full-time personal assistant at a cost that allows the average professional to seek this executive service. Imagine how your productivity can change when you go form a harried overtaxed professional to a well-organized super performer. It is also now possible to buy overnight research to expand your contribution without having to burn the midnight oil. The impact of the internet is also changing how we work together; we can now easily collaborate with other knowledge workers both within and outside of our company. All of these fuel the pace of innovation and change.
- The cost of manufactured goods will continue to fall, like agriculture fell in the past century as automation reduces the cost by reducing the labor. Manufactured items will become a smaller and smaller part of our GDP. Unless the developing world can establish a consumer base their newfound manufacturing infrastructure may be impossible to sustain.
- The public education system in America has fallen behind advanced nations worldwide. Don't count on the government to fix the problem. Be proactive, take control, as a student be better than the best, make learning a lifelong quest. If necessary, hire a tutor. As an adult, give your knowledge to your children or become a local school volunteer, keep learning.

- America's economy is the largest in the world
- We do have problems – #1 is our workforce doesn't match the opportunities. Unfortunately, re-education can be difficult for the displaced workforce. The learning skills necessary to switch careers have become stagnant from disuse. Even so, give it a shot or consider choosing a whole new direction. India's recent innovation is to avoid multi-year education for high-tech manufacturing they now focus education to pinpoint the specific skills needed and reeducate as needed.
- There are more opportunities in the USA than anywhere else (high-end management and professional jobs and low-end service jobs)
- Seize the moment, pick a direction, grab a piece of the dream.
- The market of potential customers grows with each passing month.

3. Population Explosion

I live in a lightly populated area of the northern mid-west. In the next 50 years I don't expect to see locally or even in the USA a large impact from the population explosion. Yes the population will grow modestly here but the explosion will be elsewhere. The impact we will see will be indirect. A world pushed to the limit by high demand for fuel, food, and water. In 2011 we reached 7 billion people on this planet. The growth in the last 200 years has been geometric but it is expected level off a bit by 2050 at an estimated 9.2 billion. Just another 2.2 billion souls, doesn't sound too bad. We deal in billions all the time when we talk about the federal debt. Well a billion people are a lot, and another 2.2 billion will be a disaster. If you think the level of suffering is a human travesty today, you will be appalled in a few short years.

With rising prices, we will see the increase of self-sufficiency. The gentleman farmer won't raise a few livestock and plant a garden for fun but to make sure he doesn't get caught short of necessities.

To understand how much resource demand a billion more people put on this planet think of it this way, for each person in that extra billion to have 10 gallons of fresh water a day for consumption, sanitation, bathing and washing of clothes requires 3.6 trillion gallons of fresh water per year. When you talk about each of the billion burning a single light bulb for one hour each day you need hundreds of new 300 megawatt power plants.

The population explosion will not occur in the rural countryside but in the urban mega-cities and the fastest growth is predicted in cities with populations less than 500,000. By 2050 nearly 80% of all new births will occur in Asia and Africa. We have two interesting forces at work; medicine gets better every year allowing us to live longer and as the population explosion strains our resources, birth rates will fall. These two forces will cause a general aging of the world's population. The median age is expected to raise 5 plus years by 2050. Countries able to attract skilled foreign workers will have an advantage as the world gets a bit grayer. The USA is a great place to live, the rule of law reigns supreme and the overall standard of living is high. This gives the USA an advantage in attracting talent, just because our population is aging and our education level is falling behind doesn't mean we have to watch the rest of the world whiz by us in innovation and productivity. We do need a reform of our immigration requirements to encourage skilled foreigners to join us here in the states or we lose this advantage. When you think about this trend and how it might help you plan your future, consider the services needed by both cities and the elderly. Cities need mass transportation, food, water, sanitation, rule of law, housing and entertainment diversions. The elderly lose interest in products and are more interested in services and access to good health care.

Conservation and self-sufficiency will be required as population growth strains the planet. How can this trend help you succeed? As the population grows worldwide, there will be a great strain on resources, much suffering and unrest. Some cities will fail and become a true hell on earth where crime, corruption and squalor rule the day, by the same token we will see some cities prosper and grow into great places to live, clean, efficient, and vibrant.

The big question is whether you take advantage of this trend. The center of its impact is far from American shores. As Asia and Africa place more demands on resources we will feel the impact of pollution and competition for resources. There may be products or services you can exploit. We will see a growth in humanitarian roles, crowd control products, internet sales, instruction on self-sufficiency, sales of survival gear, conservation teaching, and conservation services to just name a few. This leads right into our next high impact trend.

4. Scarce Resources

Energy, water, metals and minerals are finite resources. The known reserves and usage rates of each can be estimated. Simple math gives the number of years until we exhaust the supply of each. It is not an exact science but it does show a trend toward a serious problem for our children and grandchildren. We will find some new sources to add to the known resources and we must get better at reclaiming and reusing when we can. Despite our success at recycling, we will face some serious shortages within 35 years. Copper, zinc, lead, nickel, tin, cadmium, silver, and gold will be exhausted in 12 to 35 years. The shortest time estimate is 12 years until we will have no more silver coming from the mines. Oil is not far behind with only 40 years of supply, and unlike metal it can't be recycled. Once it becomes fuel, we burn it and it is gone forever.

The bulk of our energy comes from burning fossil fuel, (coal, oil, and natural gas), not only are we running short, we are putting so much carbon in our atmosphere that we are causing climate change. With the rising cost of gas we are starting to see the popularity of electric cars rise. But even battery power is not carbon neutral. The bulk of our electricity comes from burning coal and natural gas. Science fiction writers and many futurists see liquid hydrogen as the power of the future. A hydrogen based economy, based on extracting hydrogen from sea water could give us fresh water and no pollution problems. This day may come but it is a long way off. A lot of challenges need to be solved in both production and distribution. Government support for basic research is not near the level needed to push this alternative forward. The politics of special interest groups grounded in the status quo of fossil fuels needs to end and planet friendly intelligence needs to rule this century.

Scarce resources are a complex problem and balancing resource use against the needs of the planet is even more complex. There is no way for the resources on this planet to support all the humans at usage rates anywhere near the level of consumption in the developed world. If you have compassion for the undeveloped parts of the world you may think this is unfair. This in itself is an important lesson about success, "life is unfair". Life is a series of hardships and no amount of complaining will make them go away. Problems present opportunities for solutions. Planet abuse must stop and once we accept the reality of scarce resources we can all grow with the solutions.

It doesn't matter if you live in Africa, Asia or America you will experience hardship, how you deal with the hardship will be the measure of your success. We have no choice, using less resources and recycling everything is already a necessity. Getting everyone to understand this is the challenge.

5. Climate Change

The human industrial age hasn't been around very long in terms of the geology of the earth. Our industrial impact however has been massive. The earth has gone through cycles of warming and cooling but has not seen carbon levels like we have now since pre-dinosaur times. At this point nothing we do will stop the global warming phase we are in. The glaciers and polar ice caps will melt and flood most of the earth. The children born today will see the oceans rise at least a meter before they retire. Southern Florida and most coast line cities will be devastated. No treaty to reduce carbon emissions will have any great impact on this problem. The carbon emission from melting permafrost near the Arctic Circle alone will soon exceed mankind's contribution to this crisis.

The Arctic Ocean already has open water some months each year and for the first time in human history we have access to shipping lanes across the Arctic. Climate change of this size cannot be reversed any time soon; we will have to live with it.

Abundant resources including oil and natural gas, north of the 45 parallel will team up with milder winters to create a growing, more prosperous region in the north. As the oceans currents change and general warming trends continue "weird weather" will be more frequent. Snow storms far south, strong hurricanes, increased tornado activity will cause concern. By the end of this century we will begin to notice that there has been a population migration north. This is not only because the climate will be more agreeable but the impact of "weird" weather will be less.

If you would like an in-depth review of this serious problem try the 2010 book "The Flooded Earth" by Peter D. Ward. Professor Ward paints a picture that may make you cry but he does offer some insight on how to lessen the impact of climate change.

6. The Individual

This particular trend may be the trend that can most impact success. Many forces are at work in the world and they all add up to big impact on small groups of special interests. Instead of being a controlled "Orwell" society we have become a world where people matter and can express themselves. People have choices and because of the connected world we live in they can exercise those choices and link up with like-minded people.

Niche markets have become an important part of the global economy. If you can recognize and exploit them, they can bring you unbelievable success. A 2007 book revised in 2009 by Mark J. Penn – "Micro Trends" identifies over 70 trends that involve small groups of just a million or more people. Study of a book like this may give you insight on how to serve an underserved market or a special interest you would like to make a part of your life.

The important take away on this mega-trend is that the individual matters. People like specialized services; they like to have products (even custom products) delivered when and where they want them. The internet provides a link so people can be reached on a large-scale. Just because you live in the back woods doesn't mean you can't serve the globe. Even in my cozy cottage in northern Michigan I have high-speed internet.

Conclusion

My goal in this chapter was not to make up a new insight into the future but to summarize in common language, today's futurists' predictions. The bottom line is that our children, grandchildren and their kids will face challenges far beyond what our generation faced. The climate is changing, resources will become scarce and a rapidly expanding population is fighting for a piece of the global market. All along the way more and more people are choosing to do things their way.

As I read this summary I feel like taking a red pen and drawing arrows to nearly every paragraph with notes on how each trend could be exploited to help you succeed in the future. It is a bit hard to do on a paperback book. You have to take separate notes; these notes are something you should do for yourself. Think of it as an assignment.

As an example, when you read about the trend "Aging Population" make a note that says "expanding services for the elderly" and then list a few of the things that you might be able to offer. Healthcare, long-term care, tour groups, home and garden services, exercise programs etc... Meet with the elderly in your town, find out what services they use and what they like and dislike about them. Any one of these things could become your personal ticket to success. Once you have some ideas I suggest you gather your support group of friends and family and conduct a brainstorming session to flesh out the details. See chapter 8 if you have never participated in a brainstorming exercise.

If after completing this exercise you find your magic bullet, that one thing that will become the spark of your success, dig into it with a passion. Search for more detail on that trend, search for education opportunities that give you depth on the subject or service. Meet with potential customers or clients. Determine demand and feasibility. You can make a future you are proud of.

Chapter 7 (2nd Edition Bonus)- Brainstorming

At the end of Chapter 6 I talked a little about brainstorming. If you have spent much time in the business world you have probably experienced a brainstorming exercise, or two, or twenty. If not this bonus chapter may be of some value to you. It is not rocket science and it is a lot of fun.

First step is to assemble your team, it could be just your immediate family or friends or co-workers. Before you jump into products and services on how to be successful first brainstorm what success means to you and be able to write a summary no longer than a paragraph. Now go to chapter 6 and brainstorm on the six trends that are bringing big changes to our world today. List what goods or services you could offer to meet a need in this changing world.

A brainstorming session involves generating as many ideas as possible on a subject quickly. You can do it alone but it is best in a group because the group setting can generate ideas no one person would have come up with. Variations and versions of one person's idea may be expanded upon by another person. Personally I like to use 3x5 post-it notes and have one person write with a bold magic marker the ideas as folks shout them out. It also works to have everyone with their own pad of post-it notes and to write and paste them on the wall as they think of them.

Every idea should be spoken out loud. During the first stage of a brainstorming session the goal is to get as many ideas as possible up on the wall. No criticism is allowed, wild and crazy ideas are encouraged. Once folks run dry of new ideas see if the ones on the wall can be arranged into general categories. Eliminate silly ones and impossible ones. Now have each person rank the top 3 in each category. Do this by having each person put a slash mark on each of their 3 favorites in each category. Take the top ideas and brainstorm specifically on each. List the goals or steps needed to carry out the item.

In a nutshell that is brainstorming and it can be a powerful technique to explore and develop ideas. It can be fun to compare what you can do on your own verses what you can do in a group. You will be surprised how many more ideas you come up with in a group session. Quite often a stupid or crazy idea will produce an offshoot that becomes a viable alternative.

Sessions like these are where you can have some real fun while doing serious work. Remember to take the time to enjoy every minute.

~~~~~

Chapter 8 - Making your mark on the world

I promised to end this book with thoughts and advice that may take you far beyond personal success. As you plot your course through life you may be presented opportunities to use your energy and compassion to make a difference in your neighborhood, community, state or country. Maybe even make a difference for humanity across the globe.

If you see a need in your community and think you can help don't be afraid to get involved. You don't have to form your own non-profit organization to make a real difference. Although someday after you have some experience you may want to put your own stamp on some organization.

You don't have to reinvent the wheel; there are hundreds of nonprofit organizations already in existence. Search the word "volunteering" on Amazon, you will find over a dozen choices of books for as little as a penny plus shipping (used books). For example a book like "Make a Difference" by Blaustein lists over 140 nonprofit organizations. You may find one that really excites you and learn there are no local chapters. A national group that has already taken care of the paperwork hassles may be a great place to start. If you are really lucky you will find a local chapter and be able to join with other like-minded people.

The key is to decide what lights your fire. Seize the moment and make it happen. It doesn't matter if your motivator is feeding the hungry kids in your home town or Africa or educating the kids in your grade school or helping the freshmen at your college or even teaching an adult to read. If you choose to, you can make a difference. You can do it on your own or organize an entire community to make it happen. There is no limit to the possibilities. You may not earn a living by volunteering but you will find that the sense of accomplishment it provides can be a deeply rewarding experience.

Nearly two billion souls today live in desperate poverty and we will probably add another billion during our lifetime. Many people feel strongly about bringing social justice to the world, I am not one of them. The problems in the dark corners of the world are so vast I just throw in the towel and do nothing. I could rally my school or church or business to adopt a small town, drill a well, ship them food, and educate their children but I don't. I probably never will because the size of the situation is so overwhelming and I still feel strongly that charity begins at home. I believe in a God that cares for the suffering souls of the world and I leave the big picture in his hands. My focus has and will be first; my family, then village, region, state, and country. Just because the global problem is so big I can't have much impact doesn't mean a real difference can't be made right here in my backyard.

Natural disasters seem to be more frequent and devastating as freak weather becomes common. We may live in the "developed" world but we are not immune to natural disasters, poverty or the needs of the elderly. There is plenty to do right next door. Start small, sponsor a project, learn the ropes, it may help you plot a course for your future or it may become your future and life's work.

No good deed goes unpunished. I hope your punishment is the warm glow of satisfaction that comes from making a difference in someone's life.

Beware:

Getting involved and making a difference can also be heart wrenching. Maintain strong self-esteem; don't expect to solve all the problems you encounter. If all you can do is ease the problem a little, be happy that you made a difference.

This gets back to one of the concepts that has helped me survive critics in both the working and volunteer world. If I do my very best and someone (including me) finds it is not good enough then "TOUGH COOKIES" I am not going to shed a tear or worry a minute because I know I did my best with the information and materials I had available. That doesn't mean you can't dust yourself off and start over, it just means you don't have to.

One of the concepts I have always lived by is that if you see an injustice, untruth or just a plain unfair rotten deal, when it is possible, i.e... within your power, MAKE IT RIGHT.

You can't solve all the problems of the world but you can have an impact on many. Start within your immediate family; expand to extended family, friends and neighbors. If you can't help with money help with your labor or support.

Too many times people are treated unfairly in school or the workplace and no one speaks up for them. Be a voice, have some guts, don't stop with just words take action to actually correct the wrong. Not within your power? Kick it up a notch, to the next level, champion the appeal. As an outside unbiased observer your opinion will carry significant weight.

A few examples:

A tree falls in an elderly neighbor's yard. You have a chain saw but not much time. Make the time; solve their "big" problem, who knows you may even get cookies. A heartfelt thank you is worth more than anything money can buy.

A bully trashes a wimps lunch, --- share yours.

A kid on crutches is struggling with a book bag -- carry it for them even if you end up late. Anyone who punishes you for a good deed has problems of their own.

A discussion on promotions dredges up events and actions from years long past where the person did not perform up to snuff. -- refocus the discussion on present performance not past missteps.

Your kid's car is destroyed by someone at fault in the accident and uninsured. -- cover the loss, pay the deductible for them. They were wronged and you have the means to make it right.

An acquaintance is robbed of $200 and you know they can't afford that kind of loss. They may even go hungry because of it. --- Cover the loss or if you can't, take up a collection to help cover the loss or sponsor a fund raiser.

Enough examples, you get the idea. -- MAKE IT RIGHT. What you do to make a difference can define your life.

That reminds me of the Indian proverb where the chief tells his son about human nature. The chief said, "Son every human has two wolfs fighting inside, one is mean, evil and sadistic, the other is friendly, good and thoughtful." The Son asked, "Which one wins?" The chief's answer was simple, "The one you feed, son, the one you feed." Throughout life, pack mentality or even the lone evil wolf inside may lead you toward things that you will be ashamed of. Vow now to be a hero and shut off that side of human nature, don't go with the flow or in any way shape or form allow cruelty, unkindness or unfairness to exist. You will be surprised how strong the good 'wolf' grows when you become a hero.

Inner peace:

Confidence and strong self-esteem are important elements in establishing our separate self. You can grow to independent adulthood without them but the trip is much more rewarding when taken boldly. Looking back the confidence may have been misplaced and the bold belief in infallibility naïve, but they fueled the charge forward into life. Traversing life's journey and making the most of our time on earth is the key to finding meaning in life. Enjoyment of each moment is precious. There is wonder all around us. We are a miracle of life traveling at thousands of miles per hour. While sitting here concentrating on breathing in and out I am being flung around the sun, across the Milky Way and around the universe at incredible speeds. Each year our distance traveled exceeds four billion miles. I am bombarded by an ocean of "God Particles" that science speculates are the 'thing' that gives mass to every bit of matter. The fact that I think and have conscious awareness is incredible. It makes me wonder how 'aware' the rest of the animal kingdom is, and confirms what I have always known, 'we are special'.

There are days when I question time spent on things that exclusively benefit 'me', it seems much of life is centered on 'me'.

Time spent:

- watching or participating in a sporting event
- reading for education or mindless entertainment
- enjoying food or beverage
- exercising
- working toward goals
- capturing the beauty of our world in pictures and images burned into my mind

That's when I realize that these types of activities are the framework that defines my life's journey. Beyond the things that exclusively benefit me, are the love and kindness I share with others as they progress on exploring their life story.

The trials of life bring joy and sorrow, fun and anxiety. I count myself lucky that I have not faced much in the way of hardship. There has always been food on the table, support of family, a career that paid well and inner peace. My youth was not marred by abuse or discipline via corporal punishment; no bullies were big enough or stupid enough to take me on. I lived in a wonderland where prejudice didn't exist. Color and heritage differences were non-existent. Hate and the sense of unfair treatment were not present with my peers. No one had much, so even division by income levels didn't seem to come into play. At least my rose-colored glasses didn't see it. Our biggest divisions were between those interested in sports and the kids we ignored who weren't either interested or capable.

I have very few regrets and those I do have are trivial in the big picture. For years I regretted not playing more seasons of High School football. The hundreds of hours of backyard ball were a waste. At times I regretted not serving in the military but I count myself lucky that I never had to take another life or even point a weapon at a living person. I certainly don't miss the horrific injuries that so many have suffered in the service of their country. Rather than pine in respect to their contribution as a hero I feel sad for their loss. Sure freedom comes at a cost but far too often it is political bull crap that puts our children at risk. I have to think long and hard to come up with any other regrets.

At times I regretted not perusing a masters and PhD. I always felt qualified to rise to the top in corporate America and cheated that it did not happen. Looking back, the nights and weekends that classes would have stolen from my young family would only have added a distance between us. The dedication required in the top slots also would have driven a wedge into my family life. Even the levels I did achieve put stress on the family but that was usually related to travel not from bringing my job home with me. Year after year I was able to leave work at the office, and I seldom thought a second about work issues at home. Looking back I realize that lying low and earning a good solid living in the shadows kept me employed at least four or five years longer than a senior role would have. Once the mergers and takeovers began, heads at the top were the first to roll. So at the end of the corporate journey I have to say I enjoyed the ride, met and worked with many interesting people, and the coolest thing was we had to learn new things each year, the job was always changing. We all were a part of rolling out new and exciting technology in the corporate world year after year.

Now as I contemplate the meaning of consciousness it too seems like a: 'me, me, me' exercise. That's ok, my life story is rich with things that are just for me, it allows me to grow and still have a deep love for others. The quantity, quality and depth of generosity to the unfortunate of the world remains an open question and as the next chapter plays out, it is as of yet unwritten, I have always let the world at large find its own way. I have to contemplate the question; "should I do more".

I relish learning new things more than being entertained by fiction or sports but at the same time I do indulge in mindless entertainment. I embrace the excitement in living vicariously with movies and sports and try to insure that life remains fun for me and everyone who shares my space.

I am surprised at the number of examples I have experienced where friends and extended family don't share continued love. Their focus is elsewhere and they totally let go of past close relationships. While my love for friends and family may rest in inaction I like to think its depth and intensity remain unchanged. I suppose that is why indifference surprises me. A former best friend who would rather hurry home to wash the dishes left in his sink, rather than grab a bite and catch up is no longer a best friend.

We are separate people whose life story may be blessed with joy and success or crushed with disease, poverty, heartache and stress. No matter what life brings if we focus on inner peace we can do our best to experience each moment, and grow from what can be learned from it. One route to inner peace is to understand exactly what you believe about God. Belief in an all-knowing God leads us to understand that in knowing our every thought God is within our consciousness and the consciousness of every being in the universe. Though we embrace our separate life stories, there is comfort in knowing consciousness connects us all. We are one and we are separate and it is glorious. The alternative of course is taking the position of belief in no God which can be cold and lonely and lead to despair. Belief is about choices.

Just as the righteous are aghast at the thought of being connected to the evil in the inner city, the dishonesty on Wall Street or the jihad of the Taliban I would just as soon avoid the sickness, sorrow, suffering and death that is also just as much a part of the reality of life. The truth is we must embrace it all, set aside the things that hurt and seek out what brings us joy. Let the hard knocks teach us about ourselves and our world but never let them break our spirit. Maintain a safe place for the mind to escape, when the dark clouds try to envelop us. Nothing can touch you when inner peace is found. It is worth the search.

So I implore you live your life such that it won't be mourned when you go on to the next adventure. Hope that your friends and family will rejoice in your love of life and the fact that you stretched it to its limits and enjoyed each moment. Count yourself lucky if you have good friends, family and the opportunity to enjoy it all in good health for many years. The good, the bad and everything in between is what fuels life.

If all goes well with any luck by age 90 or 100 you can slide out sideways with a wore out body yelling yippee what a trip. Let's hope your friends and family can greet your departure not with tears but celebrated in a way similar to the way your birth was greeted, with joy and great expectations.

The late Jim Rohn who perhaps was the world's foremost

speaker on success once said: "We all have two choices: We can make a living or we can design a life." I hope your design can now take the past, present and future global forces into consideration and leads you to a path you can consider a success.

I leave you my last words; "Success is what you want it to be and what you make of it. It is in your hands, go forth and succeed on your own terms." No one can or will do it for you. Responsibility is squarely on your shoulders.

About the Author:. W. Michael Allen –After more than 30 years as an indentured servant Mike left corporate America in 2008 and has never looked back. He doesn't miss the 12 hour days, the hectic worldwide travel, the back to back meetings conducted all day and in the wee hours of the night to accommodate the global time differences and the most hated of all, the constant barrage of eMail. Just how do you answer 100 eMails a day with five minutes between meetings? One would think managing data centers would be pretty straight forward, keep the machines running with the highest reliability and lowest cost possible. Well corporate America is always about the next big program, enlighten and empower employees this week, right size and eliminate them next week. Don't forget while you have them on the hot seat to write up a useless performance review to keep HR happy. That career had its moments of fun and great people to work with but ended with over 10 years of outsourcing and offshoring and dealing with a lot of very stressed out employees.

Luckily Mike honed his writing skills on hundreds of technical project proposals and became adept at making a complex subject accessible to everyone. Today he tickles the keys of a laptop hoping to make a literary contribution, while watching the waves lap the shore and enjoying a post card perfect view.

He is now retired and when not golfing or skiing, he writes and speaks on success and future trends. Residing once again in northern Michigan he enjoys life with his wife (and editor) Rhonda.

Flashcards available at:

http://success21stCentury.webs.com/flashcards.htm

Check out the author's blog – ramblings on success:

http://success21stCentury.wordpress.com

Made in the USA
Charleston, SC
11 September 2013